Experiencing Computer Architecture

A Computer Hardware Guide for Software Developers

Steve Halladay

Principle Publishing
Park City, Utah

The author and publisher have taken care in preparing this book, however they make no expressed or implied warranty of any kind and assume no responsibility for errors or omissions. No liability is assumed for incidental or consequential damages in connection with or arising from the use of the information or programs contained herein.

Principle Publishing and the author would like to thank Rachel Antion for her services in editing and proofreading the manuscript for this book.

ISBN-10 0-9911927-2-9
ISBN-13 978-0-9911927-2-4
2nd Printing August 2015

Because hardware shouldn't scare software developers...

Contents

Preface

I have spent decades as a successful software engineer. From search engines to databases, compilers and mobile apps, I have built one of just about any kind of software you can imagine. While this was a wonderful career, during most of it I harbored a deep, dark secret.

It wasn't the kind of secret that polite software engineers discussed in public. In fact, most software engineers seemed to naturally avoid any topics that might lead to any hints of this secret. And yet, I sensed that many software developers shared this secret with me.

When absolutely necessary, we had euphemisms that allowed us to discuss the topic without directly referring to it – words like "boxes", "servers", and the most recent one, "the cloud". But at the end of the day, we were all afraid to approach the secret.

One day I couldn't take it any more. I had to come clean. I determined that I had carried this baggage for too many years. I had to say the thing that I feared more than the black hole of Calcutta. It was... *Hardware*! The problem I had was that I didn't understand it.

It is true that the first step to recovery is admitting that you have a problem. So once I admitted that I didn't really understand hardware, I mean the stuff that ran somewhere beneath my software, I began to heal. Hardware had been a black art, a mystical enigma that seemed beyond my reach, but I finally decided it was time to face hardware and figure out how it worked.

I had taken some classes in college where they tried to explain stuff to me, but it never really made sense. In these classes all I did was connect hardware by following a recipe, but I didn't really understand what I was doing. I kept asking myself, "What do these chips and resistors and wires and stuff have to do with a perfectly reasonable for-loop?" When I would ask hardware engineers about these issues, they would start to talk gibberish about HDL and bi-metal semi-conductive super-cooled lithium-based gate counts. Well, they probably didn't say that, but I swear that's what I heard. It just didn't make sense.

I understood a little about electricity. I could build a flashlight circuit. I could wrap wire around a nail and create an electromagnet. But I just couldn't seem to figure out what this had to do with computers.

Things finally started to change when I started to play with hobby robotics controllers like the Arduino. See, there were companies out there building inexpensive pluggable hardware pieces that allowed me to build motor controllers and use simple sensors without really having to know much about hardware. This was a gentle introduction. As I began to play with these hobby toys, I became more curious.

The more I played, the less hardware scared me. Before I knew it, hardware was beginning to make some sense to me. Encouraged by this toehold, I began to spend more time investigating how computers worked. Over time, I was able to put the puzzle together and finally make sense of what was going on – down there. The big surprise was that once I understood it, I realized it wasn't mysterious at all. Hardware is actually very simple!

Since my coming clean and reaching an understanding, I have come to realize that I am not alone in my fear of the dark art of hardware. Many software engineers have the same phobia. Recently I was attending a conference for software developers. The conference had a session on Arduino and hobby robotics. I attended the session to see what I could learn. The speaker of the session divided us into pairs and handed out Arduinos to every pair. I had played with Arduinos before, so I was comfortable, but I noticed my partner was terrified of the hardware sitting in front of us. He treated it as it if were Ebola. As I looked around the room, my partner was not alone. Many in the room had the same reaction.

The funny thing about this experience is that software developers are embarrassed that we don't understand hardware. Who knows why? Somehow we believe that people are endowed with an innate understanding of how computers work and we are somehow solely lacking. It isn't true. Very few software developers really understand how the hardware works. That's the first big misconception.

The second misconception is that understanding how hardware works is very complicated and hard to understand. As I finally started to piece things together I came to realize that it is all really very simple. The problem isn't that hardware is hard to understand. The problem is that it needs to be presented in a way we mere software mortals can assimilate.

That's what this book is for. In this book I want to present hardware to software developers in a way that makes sense. I try to present it in small and understandable steps. It isn't difficult if we take it one step at a time and understand each small step. Granted there are several steps, so we need to make sure we understand each one or we can get lost. But each step is really pretty easy to understand, so don't be afraid. I promise to be gentle.

Not only has this understanding cleared my conscience of the long-held secret, but also understanding hardware has had a liberating affect on me. I invite you to come along and join me. I invite you to come along and experience the euphoria and freedom of being able to look yourself in the mirror and honestly say out loud – I understand hardware!

This is a hardware book written for software developers. This chapter introduces computer architecture, or in other words how a computer works and what it is made of. We also investigate why we care about computer architecture. Finally, we consider the path this book will chart.

Chapter 0 – Introduction

If you are like many programmers today, you have spent thousands of hours at the keyboard grinding out code for sundry programs. These programs may cause the computer to host a website, recognize pictures of kittens or even simulate a moon landing. But if you are indeed like most programmers, you may have no idea how the computer hardware allows you to do these tasks.

Programmers haven't always been clueless about how the hardware of the computer actually works. Back in the 1940's, the six women who programmed the ENIAC, which is considered to be the first general-purpose computer, knew a great deal about how the hardware worked. These women would program the computer by literally re-wiring the machine. The machine was made up of a set of electric adding machines with plugboards – like the old telephone switching centers. To program the ENIAC, these women would plug wires between the adding machines in such a way as to allow the computer to calculate ballistics trajectories. It would take approximately a week to set up a program in this way, and once programmed, the machine would churn out ballistics tables for several weeks. All together, the computer would be reprogrammed about once a month.

Things have come a long way since the ENIAC, but the notion of programming is essentially the same. When we program, we are trying to create a metaphor or a model to represent some reality. The programmers of the ENIAC used wires and adding machines to create a model representing the reality of a missile flying through the air. Programs today also create a model to represent some reality. In the case of the Angry Birds program, the model and the reality are essentially the same as that used by the ENIAC.

However programs can represent other realities. For example, programs like word processors can model paper documents. Self-driving car programs model automobile drivers, and email systems model interpersonal communications.

The one thing that has changed in programming since the early days is the conceptual distance between the program and the reality it models. The conceptual connection between the ENIAC's wires and the reality of the missiles in the air is quite obtuse. It required very brilliant minds to understand the isomorphism between these two systems.

Today, the gap between the computer model and its corresponding reality is much more narrow. We now program using objects that correspond directly to things in reality. For example, a banking system might have objects to represent accounts, transactions, dates and locations. It is not too difficult to see the correspondences between these objects and their counterparts in reality.

As computer technology has evolved, we have built tools that allow us to focus less on the hardware and more on the reality we are modeling. This makes programmers much more productive, but this evolution has the side effect that many programmers no longer understand how a computer works at a basic level. This is not necessarily a bad thing, many programmers have long and successful careers without understanding anything about how the hardware works.

So why should programmers want to understand how computer hardware works? Well, there are several reasons why this may be helpful.

First, inquiring minds want to know. It's a bit like watching a magician perform a magic trick. The trick itself is fun, but many of us want to understand what makes the trick work. Where did the rabbit come from? How can a person who appears to be sawn in two still wiggle his or her feet? How did the magician know that I was thinking of the ace of spades? It is difficult to observe a magic trick and not have these types of questions. Similarly, we might ask ourselves, when I write certain lines of code, how does that make the alien move across the screen?

Second, if we understand how the underlying hardware works, we are better prepared to interact with it. This understanding may help us make our code more efficient or effective. Understanding how the hardware works may allow us to write clever programs to take advantage of hardware capabilities or even prevent security attacks.

As we move up levels of abstraction, we have a tendency to become less efficient. Programmers today who work with class libraries may not understand how a certain container works, let alone the underlying hardware. As a result, software becomes lethargic. For example, decades ago computers with much less processing power had operating systems that could boot much faster than the operating systems of today. One would think that the faster processors of today would cause our current operating systems to boot instantaneously. Why is this not the case? Certainly the useful work that today's operating systems do in the boot sequence is greater, however, it may also be that the increased levels of abstraction have added undue overhead. This overhead can result from a lack of understanding about how the underlying systems operate.

Third, the same principles and ideas that allow the hardware of a computer to work can also be used in other domains. For example, when you understand how to design the circuitry of a Boolean expression, you can see how these same ideas may be applied to machine learning. Or, the notions used to verify your working circuitry form a framework that explains a perspective on software testing. Learning to diagnose hardware problems helps us know how to diagnose software problems. We can appreciate hardware testing strategies that we may leverage into software testing strategies. And the list goes on.

Finally, when we understand how computer hardware works, we become confortable with digital electronics. This opens up many fun areas such as systems control and robotics. Today there are many inexpensive electronic parts and components available to hobbyists. It is surprising what fun things you are able to do with even a limited understanding of digital electronics you receive by understanding how a computer works.

This book will help you get this understanding. Here's how we will approach the topic:

Chapter one will describe the general computer architecture in terms of its major components. This overview will help us understand the major functions we will be building throughout the remainder of the book. Given this map of the computer, we can dive into the details of the components. Chapter one doesn't have a project like the remaining chapters, but offers broad-brush strokes to guide our thinking during the other chapters with their associated projects.

Although chapter one begins with a top-down overview, chapter two starts our bottom-up journey by jumping to the very foundation of computers. Chapter two explains the basics of electronics. This chapter does delve into a little bit of theory, but only enough to lay a working foundation. Not to worry – there will be no heavy math equations or strange symbols. Chapter two will stick to basic ideas in simple English.

Chapter three builds on the concepts of chapter two by introducing the transistor. We will learn how to use transistors to build NAND gates, which are the elementary building blocks of the entire computer.

Chapter four investigates using NAND gates to build the circuitry of all of the basic Boolean operations. By employing Boolean logic, we move up level of abstraction beyond the transistor and the NAND gate.

Chapter five uses the gates defined in chapter four to build circuitry for binary operations such as adding and shifting. We will also learn about multiplexors and demultiplexors. We can use these constructs to create an Arithmetic Logic Unit (ALU). The ALU is the fundamental workhorse of the computer, and chapter five shows, its operation is relatively straightforward.

Chapter six looks at circuits that have a feedback aspect. These are the circuits designers use to create memory, counters and the like.

Chapter seven uses the concepts and constructs from the previous chapters and puts it all together to form a simple computer. While this may sound overwhelming, by the time we get to chapter seven, it will become almost obvious how a computer works.

This book is a hands-on book. Each chapter presents various projects so that you can enjoy the discovery of these ideas on your own. The projects utilize a combination of actual hardware as well as circuitry simulation software.

When a project uses actual hardware, the project description will outline the necessary hardware. The hardware is inexpensive and can be obtained online for tens of dollars. The author encourages readers to experiment with the hardware as well as with the simulation software. Playing with the hardware in a hands-on manner seems to eliminate the mystery behind electronics in a way that software simulation does not. So, take time to plug some wires into a breadboard and enjoy your experience with this book!

In this chapter we take a high-level tour of the major components of a computer. This tour sets the stage for the remainder of the book in which we will build our own computer from the bottom up. There is no project at the end of this chapter, we are merely charting a direction for the remainder of the book. If you are anxious to get your hands dirty with some real circuits, feel free to skim this chapter.

Chapter 1 – An Overview of Computer Architecture

What makes up a computer? If you ask an average person to list the parts of a computer, they would probably say something like the processor, the disk, the screen, the keyboard and the mouse. While this is a correct answer at some level, this response is mainly a list of computer peripherals, or in other words, the things that attach to the actual computer.

What we will investigate in this chapter and further in this book, are the parts of the computer that constitute the processor. These subcomponents aren't as easy to see as the peripherals. In fact, with today's computers you would need to use a powerful microscope to be able to see the components we will discuss in this chapter.

But not to worry, we are less interested in actually seeing the sub-components of a processor, and more interested in understanding their functionality – what they do. Then, once we understand what the sub-components do, we will use the remainder of the book to explore how they work.

Each computer make and model may be slightly different, similar to how each make and model of a car is different. However, various makes and models of computers, as well as cars, have similarities. For example, all cars have steering wheels, brakes, lights and engines. While each of these cars' components works slightly differently, the general way they function is the same. Similarly, computers have many commonalities, even though their details can be quite different.

In this book we will study the construction of a "generic" computer. In other words, the description will not represent any specific computer. In fact, the computer we study in this book will not represent any real computer at all. Instead, this book will describe the general functioning of computers in such a way as to help the reader think about computers generally. Specific details will vary from computer to computer.

If we take a top-down view of a generic computer, the computer consists of three major pieces: a processor, memory and peripherals. Historically, designers used to connect these three types of components together on a bus (See Figure 1.1). A bus is really just a bunch of wires that are hooked to each component. The purpose of each of the individual wires of the bus is different, and we won't go into detail about this now, but the idea of a bus is that each of the components can talk to any of the others.

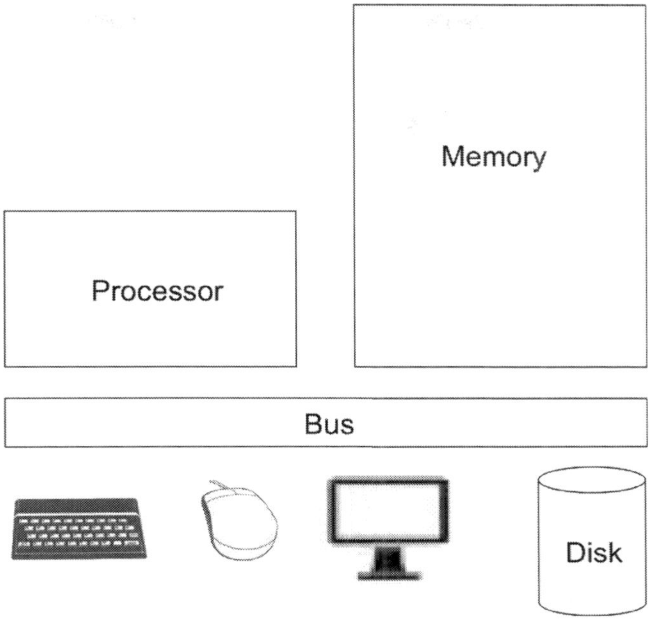

Figure 1.1. A Generic Computer Architecture.

As previously mentioned, peripherals might consist of a display, a keyboard, a mouse, a disk or even a network connection. In this book we won't go into how peripherals work. We will only note that the processor can transfer data to and from peripherals.

Let's look at each of the components starting with memory. Memory is where a computer stores its non-persistent data. "Non-persistent" means that when you turn the computer power off, the memory loses its contents. On the other hand, persistent storage, like that found in disk drives, retains the data even if we turn the power to the device off. From a programmer's perspective, memory looks like a big array of bytes. Chapter six will describe the circuitry for memory.

The processor is the part of the computer that performs calculations such as arithmetic, logical operations and controlling the movement of data to and from memory or peripherals. The processor is main area of focus for this book.

The processor may also be decomposed into subcomponents as shown in Figure 1.2. These sub-components include the ALU, Control Module (CM) and registers.

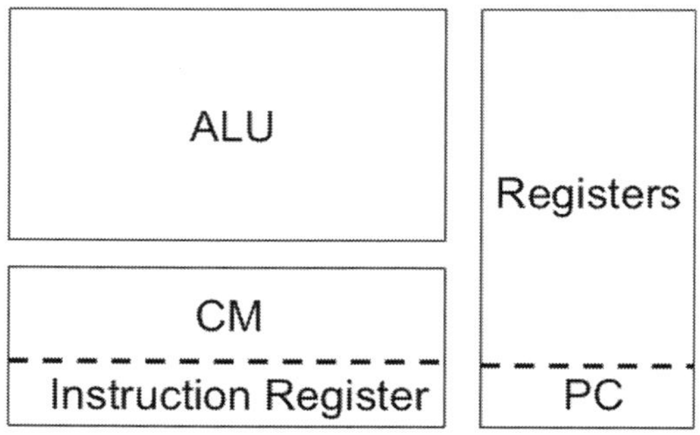

Figure 1.2. Typical Processor Sub-components.

The ALU is the part of the processor that actually performs the arithmetic and logic calculations. These calculations might include operations such as adding, subtracting and comparing numbers.

The CM is responsible for decoding instructions and moving data around within the processor. When a computer executes an instruction, the execution requires several phases. The actual phases for execution vary between processor types, but the general flow of execution has the phases shown below in Figure 1.3.

Instruction Fetch	Instruction Decode	Data Resolution	Instruction Execution

Figure 1.3. Phases of an Instruction Cycle.

Each of the phases may be broken down further into steps, however the steps will vary depending on the type of instruction.

Up to this point you may have considered processor instructions as atomic operations, or in other words, something that could not be decomposed into smaller steps. But as we see, executing an instruction requires many sequential operations. Each of these smaller steps requires a discrete amount of time. Notice also that each of the phases of the instruction must operate sequentially. So the total time to execute a single instruction is the sum of the times for each phase.

While the time required to execute a single instruction is miniscule, programs require billions of execution cycles. Because of this scaling effect, it is important to make each instruction as fast as possible. One way to speed up a processor is to streamline each phase of execution. However, one can only speed up a phase of an instruction so much. It's a lot like optimizing a program. You can find the best algorithm and write the cleanest code, but there comes a point when you really can't cut any more out of your code because it requires a minimum number of operations to do the work.

The same is true when designing circuitry. Certainly some circuits are more efficient than others, and good hardware designers will use the most efficient designs. So we might think that once we have the most efficient design we are done. However, this is not necessarily the case.

Most of today's processors overlap the instruction execution phases of operations so that while the ALU is executing the logic for one instruction, the CM is resolving the data for the next, and the CM is also decoding the instruction after that, etc. When processors overlap phases of instructions, it is called pipelining. Figure 1.4 shows a typical instruction pipeline.

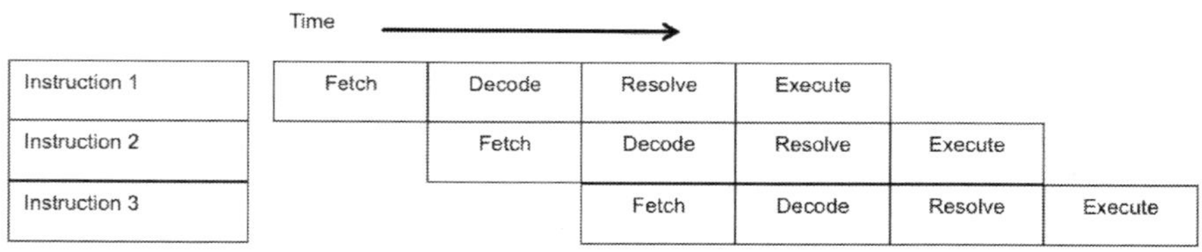

Figure 1.4. A Typical Instruction Pipeline.

While a pipelined processor design is beyond the scope of this book, one way to envision the approximate design would be to replicate the circuitry for the part of the processor that manages the various instruction phases.

The registers in the processor are storage mechanisms, like memory, that are directly accessible by the ALU. Typically the ALU cannot access memory directly, so the CM must move data from memory to register so that the ALU can operate on the data. Usually a processor will only have a handful of registers such as 8, 16 or 32.

Some of a processor's registers may have special assignments or capabilities. For example, it is common to use the lowest register as the program counter (PC). The program counter is a register that holds the address of the next instruction the processor will execute.

Imagine a processor with eight registers numbered 0-7. In such a processor register number 0 might be designated as the program counter and would contain a number representing the address of a location in memory. During the fetch phase of instruction, the CM would use the value in the PC to locate the next instruction for execution. The CM would load the value of memory as indicated by the PC into the CM's internal circuitry. This internal circuitry is known as the instruction register. The instruction register is not a general-purpose register and cannot be manipulated directly by a program.

Once the CM loads the instruction, the CM can then proceed to decode the instruction. Decoding the instruction amounts to investigating various bits in the instruction and turning on and off certain circuitry in both the CM and the ALU based on the instruction's bit values.

The processor also performs data resolution. For example, loading a value from memory into a register requires that the processor first load the address of the value and then load the value at the address. This is called *indirection* and happens during the data resolution phase.

Finally, once all the circuitry is set up and all the values are in place, the processor can actually perform the operation during the execution phase. At the end of the execution phase, the processor will have updated all the resulting register values including the program counter.

In order to understand how processors work to execute a program, let's look at a simple example. Imagine a line of C++ code that increments a variable named X as follows:

```
X++;
```

If one complies a C++ program and uses certain settings for the compiler, the compiler will generate assembly instructions from the original source code. Assembly instructions are pneumonic representations of machine instructions. As such, the assembly instructions are easier to read than machine instructions. Generally, there is a one-to-one correspondence between assembly instructions and machine instructions – that is, each assembly instruction translates into a single machine instruction. Whereas, this is not true for higher-level language instructions, as we will see shortly.

Incrementing X in C++ might translate into something like the following assembly instructions:

```
Load 1,X
Load 2,#1
Add 1,1,2
Store X,1
```

Here is how to interpret these instructions. Each instruction begins with an operation. In our example there are three different types of operations: Load, Store and Add. The number and types of operations available depend on the processor type. In this example, Load moves a value from memory to a register. Store moves a value from a register to memory. Add adds the values contained in two registers and stores the result back in a register.

Following the operation part of the assembly source lines, each instruction has arguments associated with the operations. These arguments tell the operations where to retrieve and store the values associated with the operations. Often in assembly languages, the first argument is the destination of the operation – meaning this is where the result of the operation ends up. The other arguments indicate other values necessary to complete the operation.

For example, the first instruction in the code above tells the processor to load the value at location X, which is in memory, into register 1. The second instruction tells the processor to put a constant value of one into register 2. So after executing the first two assembly instructions, register 1 contains the value of X and register 2 contains a constant one.

The third instruction in the example adds the contents of register 1 to the contents of register 2 and places the result back in register 1, overwriting the value of X that was in register 1. Finally, the fourth instruction moves the value from register 1, which is the result of the addition, to the memory location of X.

As previously mentioned, each assembly instruction corresponds to a single machine instruction. It is the job of an assembler to translate assembly instructions into machine instructions. Each machine instruction is a bit-pattern that has the same number of bits as the machine's word. The size of a word is the size of data that is convenient for a specific machine. Word sizes are typically a multiple of two bytes. For example, a word might be two bytes (16 bits) on some machines or four bytes (32 bits) on others.

Let's look at how an assembler might translate the Add instruction from our example code into a machine instruction. In order to work through this example, we will have to imagine some characteristics about our target machine. Let's start by imagining that the target machine has a two-byte (16 bit) word. Further, let's imagine that the first seven bits of the instruction indicate the type of operation the instruction is. We call these seven bits the *opcode*. We might interpret the opcode as shown:

0000000 – No-op
0000001 – Add
0000010 – Load
0000011 – Store
0000100 – Compare
...

With seven bits for the opcode, the processor could have 2^7 or 128 different types of operations.

What about the other nine bits of the word? Well, we might use three bits to represent a register number, so we could fit three register numbers in the remaining nine bits of the word. This works well for the Add operation, as it requires three different registers (i.e., the destination register and two addends). So, given these assumptions, to encode the Add operation as a machine instruction, the resulting bit string would look as shown in Figure 1.5 (spaces added to help make it readable).

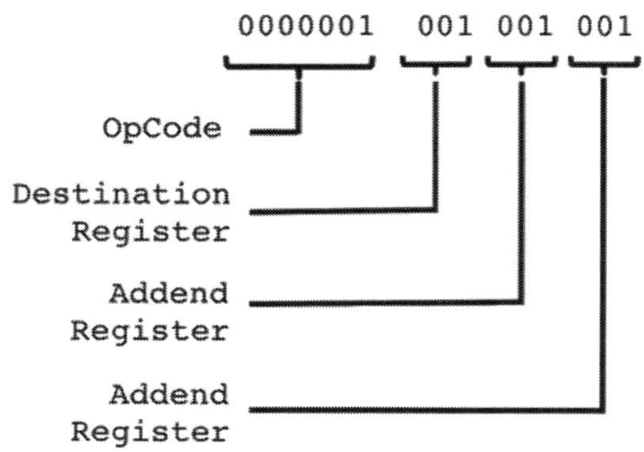

Figure 1.5. Instruction Decoding.

The processor would execute the Add instruction by following the instruction execution phases described earlier. First, the CM fetches the instruction bits from the location in memory as designated by the PC. Next, the CM decodes the op-code bits to set up the ALU for an Add operation. Additionally the CM points the ALU at the appropriate addend and destination registers based on the last nine bits of the instruction. This completes the decode phase. The add instruction requires no data resolution, so nothing would happen during this phase. Finally the ALU performs the Add operation as indicated. The last thing the CM does is to increment the PC to point at the next instruction that the processor will execute.

This description of how a processor deals with instructions, as well as the example instruction set, is greatly over simplified, but they give a flavor for how a processor operates. But, in future chapters we will fill in the details. This example also helps us see how we can map from a high-level language to assembly, and then to machine language.

In this chapter we talked about the general architecture of computers, but this was all very vague. It's time to dig into the nuts and bolts of a computer. In the next chapter we'll get our hands dirty and actually start building the basic circuitry necessary for computing.

In this chapter we will build our first simple circuit that turns on an LED. The purpose of this chapter is to familiarize ourselves with breadboarding, simple electronic components and the basic idea of electricity. Whenever we learn a new technology, it is useful to take simple, small steps and work from a known point. Once we have built this basic circuit, we will have a foundational understanding upon which we can build. This is a simple circuit, but take time to build it and become comfortable with breadboard prototyping.

Chapter 2 – Simple Circuits

There is a simple yet profound reoccurring idea in computation. Mathematicians refer to this idea by the name *isomorphism*. Theoreticians call it *reduction*, and computer scientists use the term *modeling*. All of these terms refer to this idea: if two systems have similarities, you can use one of the systems to analyze, anticipate or otherwise understand the other.

We are very familiar with the idea of modeling. We used this idea in grade school when we answered story problems like: if Alice has two apples and Bob has three, how many apples do they have together? Given such a problem, we build a simple expression like 2+3=5. The equation and the problem are two correlated systems. Since these are correlated, when we solve the equation, we also solve the original problem.

At this point you may be tired of talking about theory and you are itching to start actually doing something. So let's set the theory aside for a moment and dig in to our first project.

This first project will walk us through exactly what to do so that we become familiar with how to use these electronic parts. Later projects will leave more to our imagination.

Lets start by connecting the power source to the breadboard like the one shown in Figure 2.1. Let's first familiarize ourselves with the breadboard. The breadboard consists of lots of holes. We push the leads of components or the ends of jumper wires into these holes to connect various wires and components together.

We notice that the breadboard has two separate halves that seem to mirror each other. If we look at each of these halves from the middle out, we notice that there is a gap in the holes of the breadboard that runs the length of the breadboard. Eventually, we will place components on the breadboard by pushing-in the leads of the components so that the components straddle this gap.

We notice that the breadboard labels the columns of holes with numbers and the rows with letters. The breadboard connects the holes of the columns together such that if we insert a lead from a component and a jumper wire in the same column, the lead and the wire will be connected, but only on each side of the center gap. In other words, holes 1A-1E are connected, and holes 1F-1J are connected, but holes 1E and 1F are NOT connected. The same is true for each of the 63 columns shown in Figure 2.1 (Note: your breadboard may be shorter, but it works basically the same way).

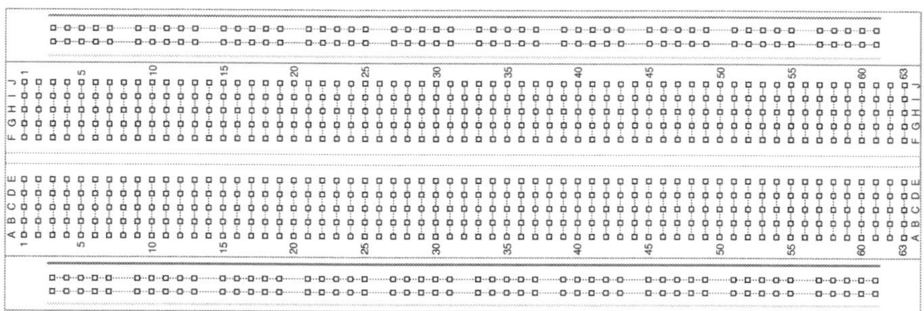

Figure 2.1. The Breadboard.

We notice that there are also two rows of holes that run along the top of the board and two rows of holes that run along the bottom. All holes in a single row are connected, but holes in separate rows are not. Even though there are slight gaps in each row at an interval of every five holes, the holes on each side of the gap *are* connected. The gap just makes it a little easier if we need to keep count. We will generally use these rows at the top and bottom for our power source connections.

If you have played with electricity some, you may be aware that there are two categories of electricity referred to as alternating current (AC) and direct current (DC). While it may not be a perfect analogy, it may be helpful to think of electricity as water flowing through a hose. Direct current is like water that flows in a single direction through a hose, whereas alternating current is like water that flows one way for a short period and then reverses direction for a short period. The current coming from the wall is AC, but for digital logic we will work only with DC. If you have a power supply that plugs into the wall, the power supply converts the AC to DC. If you are using batteries for your project, the batteries supply DC.

To connect your power source to the breadboard, you will want to place the leads for the power source in separate rows on the outer edge of your breadboard. On most breadboards these rows have a red line running along one row and a blue or black line running along the other. Your power source also has a positive lead and a negative lead. By convention, red means positive; so connect the positive lead from your power supply to the red row of holes on either the top or bottom of the board. Connect the negative lead to the row with the blue or black line.

It is important that you do not connect the positive and negative lead in any way that they have a direct connection. Doing so would create a short-circuit. If we short-circuit a battery power source, we will run the battery down very quickly, and if we create a short-circuit with a power supply, we could damage the power supply.

Next let's place each of the components on the board. Let's start with the LED. The acronym LED stands for Light Emitting Diode. When we run current through an LED it lights up, but there are a few things to know about LEDs before we try to do this.

If you have ever created a simple circuit like that of a flashlight, you know that all you have to do to get the light to turn on is to connect one side of the light bulb to one lead of a battery and the other side of the light bulb to the other side of the battery. While this works for light bulbs, it doesn't quite work this way for LEDs.

Diodes are a type of electrical component that lets current only flow in one direction. LEDs are diodes that give off light when current is flowing through them. So if we want the LED to light up, we need to connect them into the circuit correctly.

If we look at the LED closely, we notice that the LED has two leads, and that one of the leads comes from a side of the LED that has a flat edge as shown in Figure 2.2. Notice also that Figure 2.2 labels the lead near the flat side as the *cathode* or the negative lead. The other lead is the *anode* or the positive lead.

Some LEDs do not have a flat side. In this case how are we to know which side is the cathode and which side is the anode? In this case, the shorter lead is the cathode and the longer is the anode.

Some components like LEDs have a positive side and a negative side. Other components such as light bulbs do not. When a component has a negative side and a positive side, we say that the component has *polarity* – which just means we need to make sure we connect the positive and negative sides appropriately.

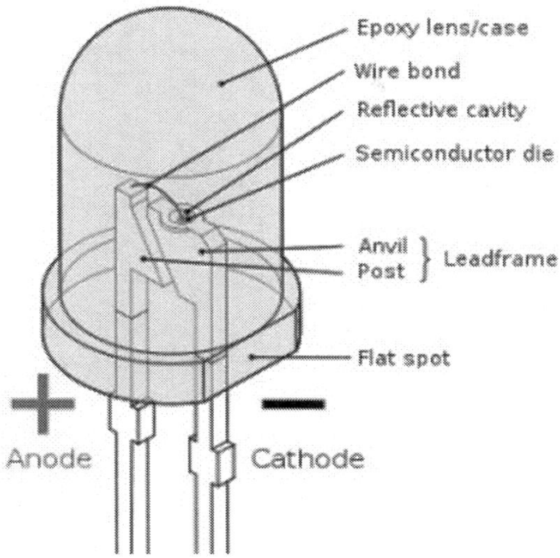

Figure 2.2. LED.

Place the LED on the breadboard so that it straddles the center gap. We can now connect the cathode side of the LED to the negative lead on the power supply by placing a jumper wire in the same column as contains the LEDs cathode, and the other end of the jumper wire to the negative row of the power source. Leave the anode of the LED for now and we'll come back later and connect it.

Next let's place the resistor on the breadboard straddling the center gap. Resistors look like tiny hotdogs with a wire sticking out of each end. Unlike LEDs, resistors have no polarity, so it doesn't matter which lead goes on which side.

If we look closely at resistors, we notice that they have several stripes of various colors painted around their bodies. The color and the placement of these stripes tell us something about the type of resistor we have. But in order to understand what the stripes mean, we need to understand a little bit about the theory of electronics. Don't worry; we'll keep it short and light.

As we mentioned earlier, we can think of electricity as water flowing through a hose, but water flowing through hoses can occur in different ways. For example, children playing in the summer might use a garden hose to spay each other for fun. Firefighters might also use a hose to disperse vast amounts of water and smother flames. If we force water through a hose with enough pressure, we can actually use the water to cut through solid granite.

What makes the difference between these various uses of water running through hoses? There are really three parameters affecting how we can use water and a hose. These parameters are the diameter of the hose, the length of the hose and how much pressure we apply to the water in the hose. If the hose has a large diameter, the hose has the potential to move a lot of water. If the hose is very long, the water is much harder to push because longer hoses offer greater resistance. And if we increase the amount of pressure on the water in the hose, we can move more water past a point in the hose more quickly.

Electricity works a lot like water. Specifically, we have three parameters that fundamentally affect electricity. These parameters are force, current and resistance and they are interrelated. It is important at this point to understand each of these parameters. Here are some intuitive definitions to help us understand these parameters:

- Force – the amount of pressure applied to electrons
- Current – the number of electrons that pass by a point over some duration
- Resistance – the drag on electrons

These three factors are interrelated. If we increase the force, the current will increase. We can think of this as pushing harder on the electrons to force them through the circuit.

Similarly, if we leave the force constant, but increase the resistance, we can expect the current to decrease. In other words, the electrons have to fight harder to make their way through the circuit. Alternatively, if we leave the force constant and decrease resistance the current will increase. This would be like greasing the path for the electrons so they could slide easily through the circuit.

The relationship between these three factors is the most fundamental idea of electronics and it is called Ohm's Law – named after a German physicist Georg Ohm who discovered this relationship around 1827. Ohm captured the relationship in the following simple equation:

> $E = I * R$
> Where E is electro-motive force (Force),
> I stands for intensité which means Current, and
> R is Resistance

The variables names that Ohm chose are a bit unfortunate for English speakers today, but these variable names seemed to have stuck as the standard, so we need to be aware of what they mean so that we can communicate with others.

We measure E or Force with units called *Volts*. As a result, some people also refer to this force as *Voltage*. We measure Current with units called *Amperes*, often shortened to Amps. And we measure Resistance with units called Ohms.

Now, back to our resistor in our LED circuit. The purpose of a resistor in a circuit is, strange enough, to increase resistance – duh! In our LED circuit we need to increase resistance so that our LED doesn't burn up. If we just use our LED without a resistor in the circuit, too many electrons will pass through the LED too quickly and cause it to get too hot. So, the resistor adds enough resistance to protect the LED.

Remember the stripes around the resistor? These stripes indicate how much resistance the resistor will introduce into the circuit in terms of the number of Ohms. There are three (and sometimes four) stripes on the resistor. Each stripe can be a different color. There are ten possible colors for each stripe where each color represents a different digit. Here is the mapping:

0 - Black
1 - Brown
2 - Red
3 - Orange
4 - Yellow
5 - Green
6 - Blue
7 - Violet
8 - Gray
9 - White

The first two stripes represent the first two digits in the number of Ohms. The third stripe indicates the number of zeros append to the first two digits. Here are some examples and their associated resistance values:

- Red, Red, Red – 2.2K Ohms
- Green, Blue, Yellow – 560K Ohms
- Black, Brown, Black – 1 Ohm

Some resistors will have a fourth stripe. In this case just treat the third stripe as a third digit and the fourth stripe indicates the number of zeros.

There is usually an extra stripe on the other end of the resistor that is either gold or silver. This stripe indicates the tolerance of the resistor. If this stripe is gold, the resistance of the resistor may vary as much as +/- 5%. If the stripe is silver, the resistance may vary by as much as +/- 10%.

The size of the resistor we use to protect the LED ought to be something like a 1K-Ohm resistor. Larger resistance values may cause the LED to be a bit dimmer, but they won't hurt anything. However, if the resistance is too small, we could damage the LED. By the way, instead of spelling out the word Ohm, people may use the symbol Ω instead, but it means the same thing.

Let's recap where we are in our project at this point. We have connected the positive lead of the power source to the breadboard to a red row on the breadboard and the negative lead is connected to a blue row. We have a jumper wire coming from the blue row of the breadboard to the flat side (or short side) of the LED. We have a resistor straddling the center gap, but we have not yet connected it to anything.

At this point let's connect a jumper wire from the anode of the LED (the non-flat side or the longer lead) to one of the sides of the resistor. As we mentioned, the resistor has no polarity, so it doesn't matter which side we choose.

Notice that the electrons in our circuit will flow from the negative lead of the power source, through the LED and then through the resistor. There is no other path for the electrons to take. When there is only one path through some components, we say that the components are connected *in series*. The alternative to connecting components in series is to connect them *in parallel*. When we connect components in parallel, electrons have branches where they may take various paths. We'll discuss series versus parallel later in the book.

Also, notice that we said the electrons flow from the negative lead to the positive lead. This seems counter intuitive. It would seem more natural for electrons to flow from the positive lead to the negative lead, but it isn't so. In fact, it took researcher some time to realize this, and by the time they did realize the direction of flow, people had created symbols based on the belief that electrons flowed from positive to negative. Therefore, some of the symbols you will see in schematics, etc. may be counterintuitive.

The next step in building our circuit is to connect the switch in series with the rest of the circuit. We can place a push button switch so that it also straddles the center gap on the breadboard. The switch has leads on two sides. Position the switch over the gap so that the leads that come out of the same side of the switch are on the same side of the gap. If your switch doesn't want to stay in the holes, you can use some needle nose pliers and carefully straighten out the pins. Now, run a jumper wire from the unconnected side of the resistor to one side of the switch.

Note that switches, like resistors, do not have polarity, so it doesn't matter which side we connect the jumper to. Finally, connect a jumper wire from the other lead of the switch (use the one that is on the same side of the gap, but is not connected to the previous jumper wire) and connect the other end of the wire to the positive side of the power source. Note that the switch has four leads. Two of the leads are connected to one side of the switch and the other two are connected to the other side of the switch. It really doesn't matter which of the two leads you use as long as you get the correct side of the switch. If you managed to get the jumper wire connected correctly to the switch, you're done.

If you have connected the circuit correctly and your power source is supplying power to your circuit, you should be able to push the button and see the LED light up. Figure 2.3 shows all the connections of the final circuit.

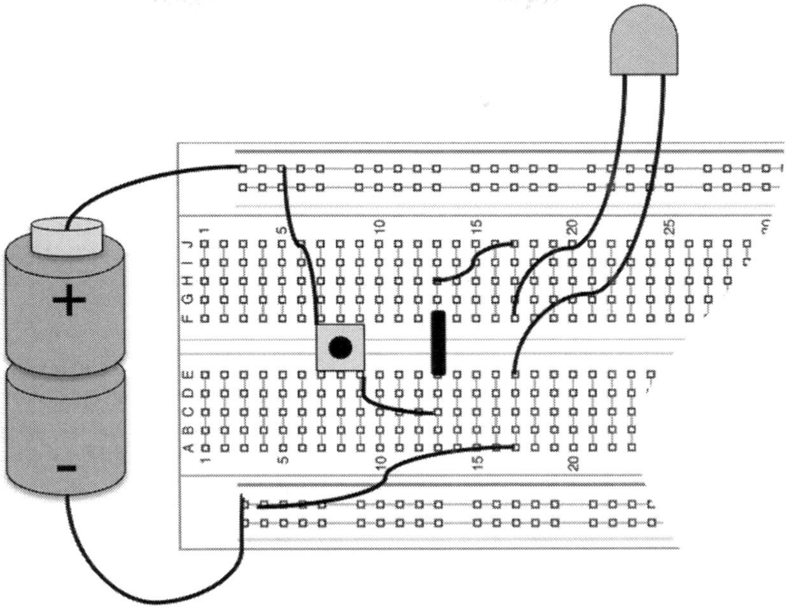

Figure 2.3. LED Pushbutton Circuit.

Should your circuit not operate correctly, here are a few tips to consider. First, stay calm and assure yourself that there is a logical explanation. We have a tendency to become very anxious when things don't seem to work and we are working with an unfamiliar technology. But realize that the technology is not magic – it's logical and you can reason your way through the problem.

Now, systematically work through the schematic, looking at each connection. For each of these connections, make sure the connection is secure and that the connection is correct. Pay special attention to the polarity of the power source and the LED. If you have carefully verified the entire circuit this way, there is a high probability that your switch is not connected correctly. A symptom of the switch being connected incorrectly is that the LED either stays on all the time, or stays off all the time.

Another possible problem that can cause a non-working circuit is if the LED polarity is incorrect. Check to make sure you connected the anode and cathode as previously described.

Finally, the only other likely problem might be that you accidentally connected the LED directly to power without having a resistor in series. It is possible that you damaged the LED. Try another LED to make sure this is not the issue.

Sometimes pictures like the one in Figure 2.3 are somewhat imprecise, especially if all we want to extract from the image is how to connect the components. At the same time, some sort of picture seems much easier to understand than an English description. What we would like is something like a picture, but more precise. Circuit designers have come up with just such a mechanism. They call them *schematics*.

A schematic is a symbolic representation of a circuit that is intuitive like a picture, but a bit more precise. In schematics we represent components with specific symbols, and connections with lines. Figure 2.4 shows the schematic for the same circuit we represented in Figure 2.3.

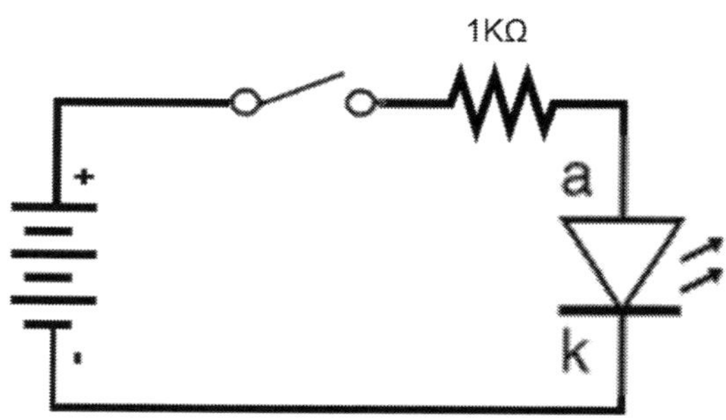

Figure 2.4. LED Pushbutton Schematic.

Starting on the left side of the schematic in Figure 2.4, we see the symbol for the power source. In this case the power source is a battery. The schematic symbol indicates the polarity of the battery with the plus sign (+) at the top, and the minus sign (-) at the bottom of the symbol. If we follow the line from the negative lead of the battery, we find that it connects to the symbol that looks like a triangle with a line under it. This symbol is the LED symbol – we can see the arrows pointing away from the triangle indicating the LED emits light. The schematic indicates the polarity of the LED with an 'a' to indicate the anode and a 'k' to indicate the cathode (yeah, we realize cathode is not spelled with a K, but this is the convention).

As we move counterclockwise from the LED, we see the jagged symbol that represents the resistor. Note that the schematic indicates that this is a 1K Ohm resistor. Finally, just to the left of the resistor is a symbol for a switch. The two terminals of the switch are not connected by the diagonal line indicating that the switch is *open*, meaning that the circuit will not be complete until we push the button.

At this point we have built our first real circuit and have learned about some electrical theory along the way. Those who are paying careful attention may be wondering what any of this has to do with the discussion that opened this chapter – namely modeling?

We can use our first circuit to try and create an analog to Boolean logic. To create this analog, imagine a Boolean function with one input and one output. For this Boolean function, if the input is true, the output is also true. If the input is false, the output should be false. We call this the *identity* function. It follows the truth table shown in Figure 2.5.

Input	Output
True	True
False	False

Figure 2.4. A Truth Table For the Boolean Identity Function.

Now, imagine that our circuit represents this Boolean function. The pushbutton is the input and the LED is the output. When we push the button, it is as if we input a true value to the Boolean function. When we release the button, it is as if we input a false value to the Boolean function. When the LED lights up, the output of the function is true and when the LED is dark, the output of the function is false. In this way, our circuit perfectly replicates the behavior of the Boolean identity function.

Admittedly, this seems very simple, but this isomorphism, or in other words, this model lays the foundation for all of our electrical computing. To generalize this model a little further, instead of saying that the LED emitting light represents a true output, we could just as easily say that when the circuit has a voltage, the output is true and if the circuit has no voltage the output is false.

We use the metaphor of voltage or no voltage to represent true and false. Sometimes we can also use it to represent 1 and 0. You may be aware that voltage in a circuit may vary. For example, our previous circuit operates at 5 volts. So we call 5 volts true, and 0 volts false. What happens if we had, say, 2.5 volts? Would that represent true or false?

The type of electronics we will be studying in this book is *digital* electronics. Digital electronics means that we don't consider values in between 5 volts and 0 volts. We make sure to design our circuits so that they operate in ranges very near to 0 volts or 5 volts, but not in between.

There is another branch of electronics know as *analog* electronics. In analog electronics, designers concern themselves with many different voltage levels. The problem with analog electronics for computing is that things get very complicated and difficult to reproduce. If a circuit uses a component that is slightly off, then the results of analog computation can be off as well. Therefore, analog devices often require special tuning to keep the values within tolerances. With the number of components needed to perform computation, the tuning would become unwieldy.

So there we have it. We are now armed with enough foundational understanding to start to build more sophisticated circuits that can do more things. In the next chapter we will build circuits to represent more sophisticated Boolean functions. Then with these functions we will be in a position to begin building computational mechanisms.

Project: Build a Push-button LED Circuit

This first project will be very simple, but it will give us a starting point for thinking about computation and familiarize us with using a breadboard. The goal of this first project is to build a simple circuit to light an LED when we push a switch. Connect the components using jumper wires as described in the chapter.

For this project we need the following parts:

- 1 breadboard
- 1 power source (either a wall wart or a battery supply pack)
- 1 pushbutton switch
- 1 LED
- 1 resistor
- 4 jumper wires

Here we will introduce what a transistor is and show how to use transistors to create a NAND gate. We note that transistors are electrical components, whereas NAND gates are Boolean logical constructs. So an important aspect of this chapter is how we move to a higher level of abstraction. We may want to take time to build each of the circuits along the way in this chapter to solidify each step towards the NAND gate, but in the least, we should be sure to experiment with the final NAND gate circuit.

Chapter 3 – The NAND Building Block

There are two big secrets that make electronic computation possible. The first of these big secrets is that all computation boils down to simple functions – or in other words, mechanisms that have inputs and outputs. In fact, for digital computation, these functions may be limited to Boolean and binary functions.

The second of these secrets we call *abstraction*. Abstraction is where we hide the complexities of a system so that the system appears to be as simple as its interface – its inputs and outputs. Abstraction allows us to manage complexity – to be able to understand and navigate complex systems. We can dive into the nitty-gritty details of some subsystem, but become unconcerned by those details as we move to a higher level of abstraction. Then, at the next higher level, we can consider another set of details and so forth.

We will use both of these secrets throughout this book. In the previous chapter we built the circuitry of the simplest of all Boolean functions – the identify function. In this chapter we will build on the idea of the identity function and create the basic building block of computation.

In the following chapters, we will apply abstraction to the basic building block to build fundamental Boolean operations. Then we will apply abstraction again to build higher-level digital functions. Finally, we will apply abstraction to these higher-level digital functions to create an ALU and processor like the ones described in chapter one.

Let's start by considering the circuitry we built in the previous chapter that created the Boolean identity function. Recall that the Boolean identity function just outputs its input. We built this function using a circuit that had several components connected in series.

For our next project, let's look at a circuit that has a parallel path. We can create this circuit by modifying the circuit we built in the previous chapter. First, let's imagine what would happen if we took the previous circuit and removed the switch. To remove the switch, we connect the positive lead from the power source directly to the resistor where the switch used to be. Figure 3.1 shows the schematic for this circuit.

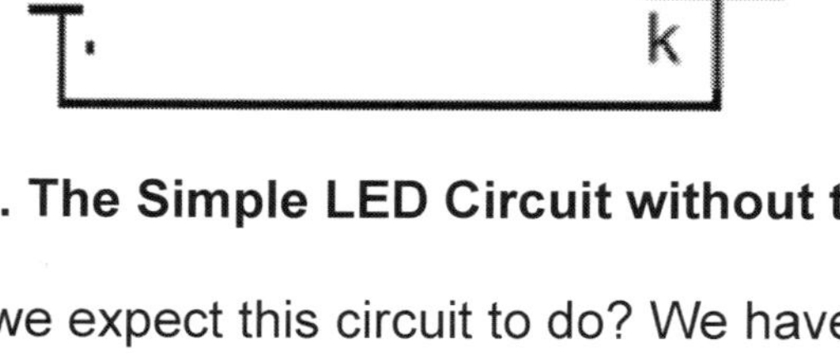

Figure 3.1. The Simple LED Circuit without the Switch.

What would we expect this circuit to do? We have essentially replaced the switch with a wire, so it's as if the switch were always closed. Previously, when we closed the switch, the LED illuminated, so we would expect the LED in the circuit in Figure 3.1 to remain constantly illuminated. Try it out and see what happens.

It was pretty easy to figure out how the circuit in Figure 3.1 would behave, but let's take a look at one that is a little more complicated. What if we take the circuit in Figure 3.1, and we add a switch *in parallel* with the LED as shown in Figure 3.2? How do we expect this circuit to behave?

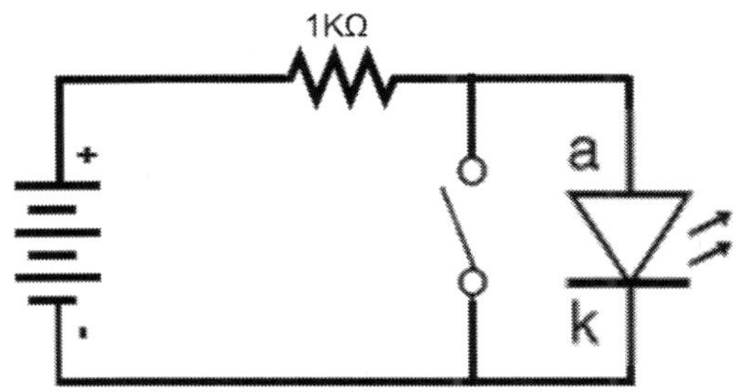

Figure 3.2. The Circuit with the Switch in Parallel.

Once you think you know how this would behave, build the circuit and test it out.

If we think about the circuit in Figure 3.2 a little, we can see that when the switch is open, the circuit will behave exactly like the circuit in Figure 3.1 – when the switch is open, the two circuits are the same and the LED is illuminated. However, the question becomes, what happens when we close the switch?

If you have built the circuit and tested it, you know that when you push the button and close the switch, the LED turns off. Why does this happen? Well, when we close the switch, we give the electricity another path that it can take. We need to ask ourselves, which path is easiest for the electricity to follow? Or, in other words, which path has less resistance? It turns out that the switch, when closed, has no resistance – or at least no more resistance than a wire (which is very small). However, the LED does have some resistance (not much, but more than the switch). Therefore, the electricity travels through the switch and avoids the LED, which causes the LED to turn off.

Now let's think about what Boolean function this new circuit represents. When we push the button, or said another way, when we input true, the circuit responds by turning off the LED or outputting false. On the other hand, if we release the button, or input a false, the LED illuminates which indicates true. If we write this out as a truth table, the table looks like Figure 3.3. What Boolean function is this?

Input	Output
True	False
False	True

Figure 3.3. Truth Table for Boolean NOT.

As you can see from the title of Figure 3.3, this is the Boolean NOT function. The Boolean NOT function inverts its input.

So far we have only dealt with circuits that simulate Boolean functions with only one input. What if we wanted to simulate a function with two inputs? What would that circuit look like? Well, if the button represents a Boolean input, we can see that a circuit with two inputs would require two buttons.

There are lots of different functions we could model with two Boolean inputs by placing the switches in various configurations, but we can easily create one simple and very useful function by adding the second switch in series with the first switch. Figure 3.4 shows this circuit.

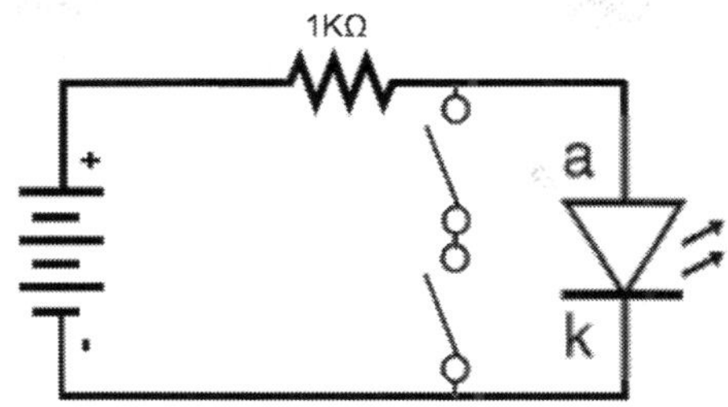

Figure 3.4. A Two-Input NAND Circuit.

If we think about the circuit described in Figure 3.4, it becomes clear how this function behaves. With both switches open, the LED is on. If we close only the top switch, the LED remains on. Also, if we close only the bottom switch, the LED remains on. However, if we close both switches at the same time, the LED goes off. Build it and try it.

What does the truth table for the functionality of this circuit look like? For this truth table we need two input columns corresponding to the two switches, and a single output column corresponding to the LED. Figure 3.5 shows this truth table.

Input A	Input B	Output
False	False	True
False	True	True
True	False	True
True	True	False

Figure 3.5. Two-input NAND Circuit Truth Table.

This function is a bit more obscure than the Identity function or the NOT function. This function is actually a composite function. It might be easier to recognize if we were to invert the outputs. Then we would see that the only time the function outputs true is when both inputs are true. We can recognize this as the AND function. But since we inverted the outputs, it's not exactly the AND function. Instead, it's the NOT of the AND – also know as *NAND*.

It turns out that NAND is significant for two reasons. First, it is extremely easy to build, and second (here's the big one), all other computational functions can be built up from various combinations and configurations of NAND. What does this mean? It means that if you tore all the logic in your computer apart, if you decomposed the logic into its atomic parts, you would find a bunch of copies of the circuit shown in Figure 3.4! It all boils down to NAND.

But in order to use these NAND circuits, we need to build them in such a way that we can have the output of one NAND circuit be the input for other NAND circuits. In order to do this, we need to introduce another component. This new component is called a *transistor*.

The first transistor was invented at Bell Labs in 1947. A transistor can be used for various purposes, but in digital electronics and computation, we use transistors as switches that we can control electronically. So, using transistors we can connect the output from one NAND circuit to the input to a different NAND circuit. We'll investigate how to do this to form the basic Boolean functions in future chapters. For the remainder of this chapter, let's look at how a transistor works and how we would plug it into our NAND circuit.

Unlike the electrical components we have seen so far that only have two leads, a transistor has three leads. These leads are called the *collector*, the *base* and the *emitter*. Figure 3.6 shows a drawing of a transistor.

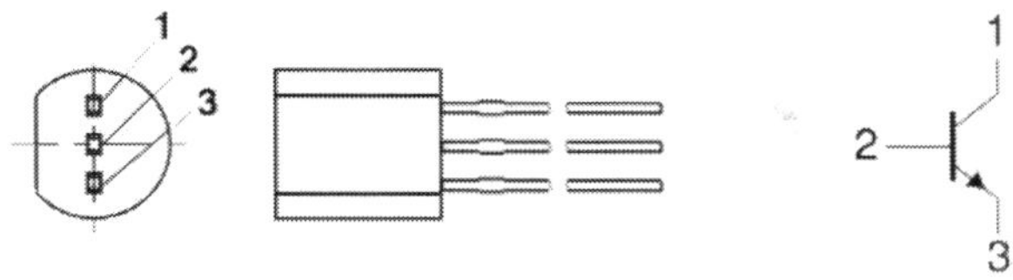

Figure 3.6. A Drawing of a Transistor, Bottom, Side and Schematic Symbol.

We see in Figure 3.6 a drawing that shows a transistor from the bottom view and from the side view as well as the schematic symbol. The Bottom perspective shows that the transistor has three leads, numbered 1, 2 and 3. We see from this bottom view that the transistor has a flat side to help us orient which lead is which. The leads are mapped as follows:

1. Collector
2. Base
3. Emitter

The side view isn't very helpful, but indicates how the leads look from the side. The schematic symbol has the leads labeled to indicate how the leads in the schematic map to the leads on the physical device.

The way the device works is that lead 1, the collector, acts like the positive side of the switch. Lead 3, the emitter acts like the negative side of the switch. Of course switches don't have polarity, but transistors do. So when we say the positive side of the switch, we mean the side of the transistor that attaches to the positive side of the power supply. Lead 2, the base, is the input that controls the switch. To close the switch, we apply current at the base.

One more point about using the transistors; often it is important to put a resistor on the base to protect the transistor, much like we did with the diode.

Figure 3.7 shows the NAND circuit with the transistors replacing the switches.

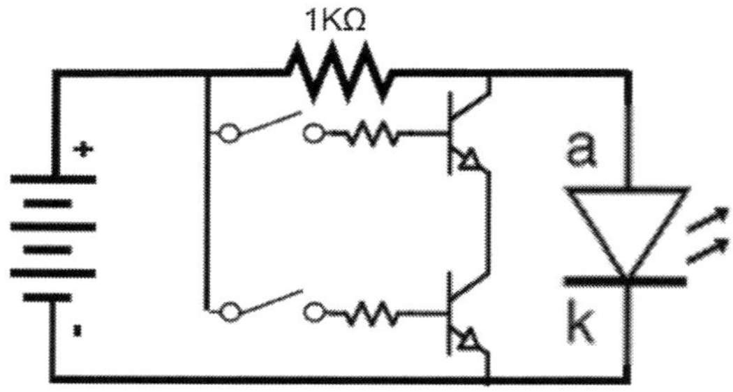

Figure 3.7. NAND Circuit with Transistors.

In the circuit shown in Figure 3.7, the three resistors can be about 1K Ω each.

We see that we still have two switches, but this time the switches perform a different logical function. Previously the switches were part of the NAND functionality. In this circuit, the switches simulate circuits feeding inputs to the NAND functionality. This is a subtle distinction, but an interesting one. So, where we see the switches in Figure 3.7, we can imagine that they could represent some other more complex circuits, each with single a output.

As we mentioned, this circuit forms the foundation for all digital computation. But we won't use all of these components in our fundamental piece – only the two transistors. In order to encapsulate this functionality so that we can reuse it as a building block, we create a new schematic symbol to represent the relevant parts of this circuit. The symbol for NAND looks like Figure 3.8.

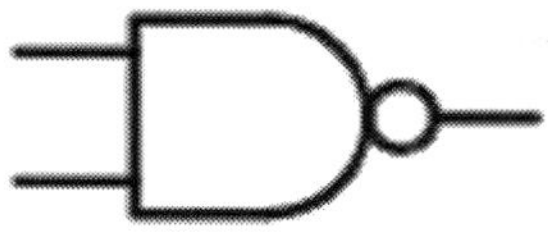

Figure 3.8. NAND Schematic Symbol.

We notice that this symbol has two leads on the left and one lead on the right. The two leads on the left are the two inputs, which are essentially same thing as the two switches in the circuit in Figure 3.7. The lead on the right is the output, which is the anode side of the LED. The schematic doesn't show the power source connections (i.e., the positive and negative power source connections at the top and bottom of the transistors). As our schematics get more complex, we don't show the power connections because they tend to clutter up the schematic. Without the power connections, the logic of the circuit becomes clearer.

In the next chapter we will investigate how to connect NAND circuits together to create more Boolean functions.

Project: Build a Two-transistor NAND Gate

For this project, we may want to build each of the circuits shown in Figures 3.1, 3.2 and 3.4. These circuits help us to build up to the circuit described in Figure 3.7. We should demonstrate and work with each of these circuits until we are comfortable with how they behave. Certainly, the circuit in Figure 3.7 is the most important.

For the circuits in this chapter, we will need the following components:

- 1 breadboard
- 1 power source (either a wall wart or a battery supply pack)
- 2 pushbutton switches
- 1 LED

- 3 resistors
- 4 jumper wires
- 2 PN2222A transistor

This chapter investigates using the NAND gate to formulate the foundational Boolean operators. We move up the electrical component food chain and familiarize ourselves with integrated circuits. The key takeaway from this chapter is that we can build all Boolean logic from NAND gates, and we have already seen how to build NAND gates from a pair of transistors.

Chapter 4 – Standard Boolean Gates

Now that we understand the NAND circuitry, which is the foundation of digital computation, we are prepared to explore the circuitry for Boolean functions. We call the NAND circuit, as well as the circuits for other standard Boolean functions, *gates*. Based on the NAND gate, we will develop a NOT gate, an AND gate, an OR gate and an XOR gate.

It would be tedious and error-prone to have to connect up the individual transistors and resistors every time we want to build a NAND gate. Plus, computers use millions of these gates, which would require a lot of space. If such were the case, you would need a forklift just to carry a cellphone around.

Fortunately, electrical engineers have been able to shrink this technology down on to silicon chips where the transistors are literally microscopic. Because we can't see the parts on the chips, chipmakers label the chips with identifying numbers. The chips we will use in this chapter are 7400 chips.

Each 7400 chip has fourteen leads, seven on each side. Figure 4.1 shows a diagram of a 7400 chip.

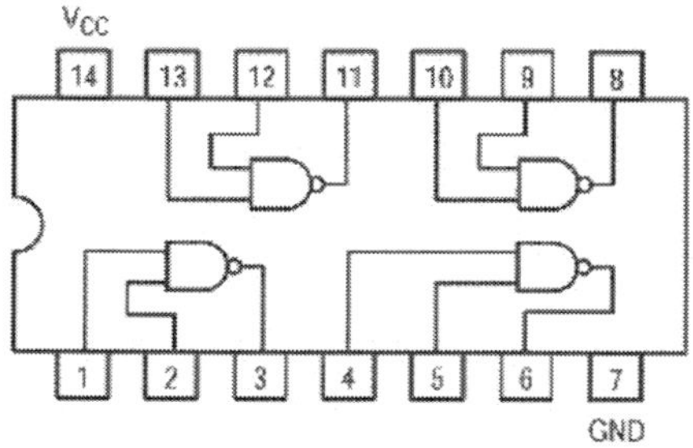

Figure 4.1. 7400 Chip Diagram.

Figure 4.1 shows a chip with a dimple on the left side. This dimple allows us to orient the chip so that we know which leads are which. Instead of this dimple, some chips indicate the first lead with a tiny circle in the chip just next to pin1.

We notice that all the pins have labels in the diagram. These labels help us identify the pins with the appropriate behavior. For example, the 7400 contains four NAND gates. Pins 1 and 2 are the inputs to the first NAND gate. Pin 3 is the output for the first NAND gate. Pins 4, 5 and 6 are the inputs and output respectively for the second NAND gate, etc.

The diagram in Figure 4.1 labels pin 7 as GND and pin 14 as Vcc. These pins are the pins that power the chip. GND is an abbreviation for the word *ground*, which means that this pin should be connected to the negative side of the power source. Vcc indicates the lead for the positive lead of the power source.

Let's investigate how these chips work. Begin by placing the 7400 chip so that it straddles the center gap of the breadboard with seven pins on each side of the gap. Also place the two switches so that they also straddle the gap. Plug one end of a 1KΩ resistor so that it connects to pin 3 of the 7400. Plug the other end of the resistor into an unused column of the breadboard. Plug the anode of the LED (the longer lead) into the same column as the second lead of the resistor so that the resistor is in series with the LED (this is to protect the LED as we discussed previously). Connect the other lead of the LED to an unused column. Place two additional 1KΩ resistors on the breadboard and connect them each between the ground and the input pins 1 and 2 of the 7400. These resistors make sure the inputs are grounded when the switches are open. Also, connect the power source to the red and blue rails on the breadboard. Finally, use jumper wires to connect the rest of the circuit as shown in Figure 4.2.

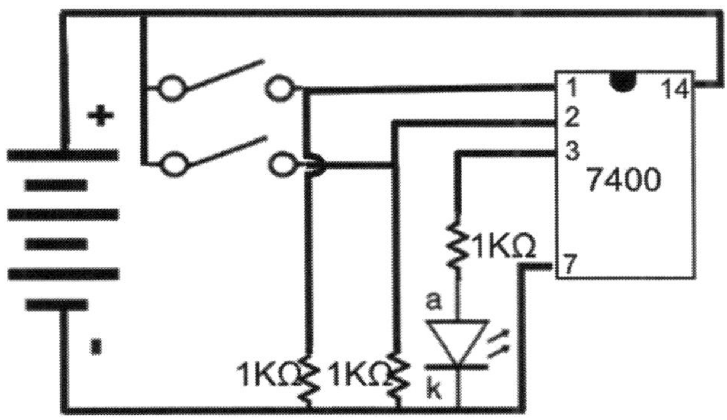

Figure 4.2. A Circuit for Demonstrating a NAND gate.

Take time to think about this. Once we connect and test this circuit, we see that it behaves like the circuit we built using transistors, except the switches are backwards (i.e., closed is now zero because the switch connects to ground). These circuits are equivalent, but the chip creates a nice abstraction that allows us to forget about the details of the NAND gate and treat it as its own component.

NOT Gate

At the beginning of the chapter we promised to create some other Boolean gates using only NAND gates as building blocks. Let's start by trying to create the NOT gate. Remember, the NOT gate has one input and one output. If you have forgotten how the NOT function works, look back at Figure 3.3. Before we go on, see if you can figure out how to create a NOT gate. As a hint it only requires a single NAND gate.

One of the challenges with creating a NOT from a NAND is that the NAND has two inputs and the NOT only has one. This is a problem, but it is also a clue. If we look back at the truth table for the NAND function as shown in Figure 3.5, we see that NAND only outputs false if both inputs are true. So what we probably need to do is replicate our one input for the NOT to both inputs for the NAND. In fact, if we tie both inputs of the NAND together, then when the input is false, the output is true, and when the input is true, the output is false. That is exactly what we want. Let's look at the circuit in figure 4.3.

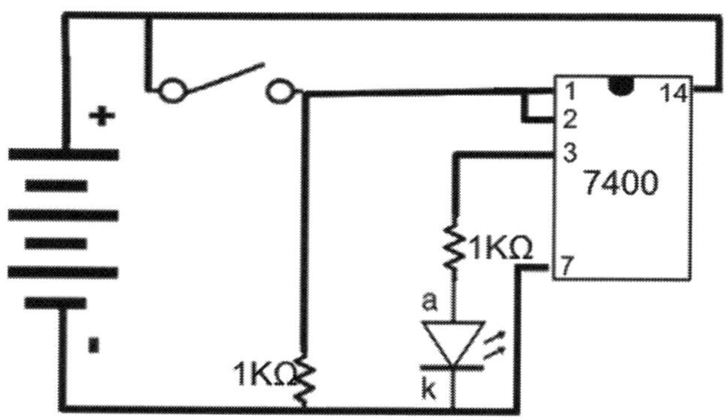

Figure 4.3. NOT Gate from a NAND Gate.

If we build this circuit and test it, we see that when we push the button yielding a zero input, the LED turns on, like the previous NOT circuit we built with transistors. Why would we build this same circuit with a NAND gate instead of just using transistors? Well, while this may waste a transistor, it is vey easy and uses a basic commodity.

What we have done here is to have moved up a level of abstraction. Now instead of thinking about electronic components like resistors and transistors, we are thinking in terms of Boolean logic. Since we have moved up a level in our thinking, our diagrams should start to reflect this level of thinking. To do this, we won't draw electrical circuits like we have to this point. Instead, we will start using Boolean schematics. The Boolean schematics only show the logical connections – we ignore the details of the circuit like resistors and power. We assume we can figure out those details. Instead we focus on the logical operations.

Figure 4.4, shows the Boolean logical counterpart to the electrical schematic shown in Figure 4.3.

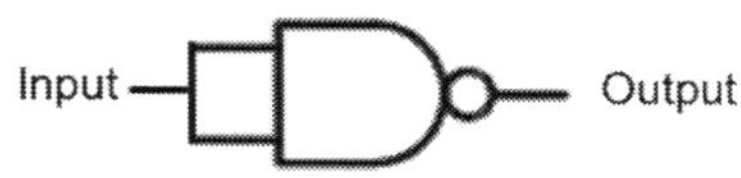

Figure 4.4. Boolean Schematic for NOT from NAND Gate.

The NOT gate, like the other gates we will build in this chapter have their own symbols as shown in Figure 4.4.

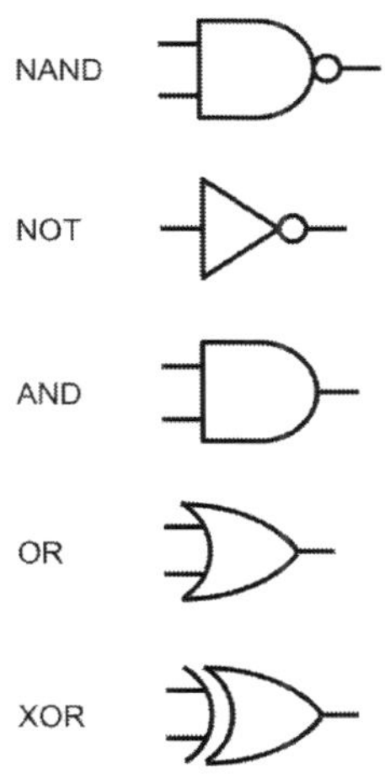

Figure 4.4. Standard Boolean Symbols.

As we derive each of these gates, we may add them to our repertoire of tools that we can use to build up further logic. If we ever want to see the NAND gate circuitry at the base of our logic, we can recursively replace the higher level symbols with their derivations until only NAND gates remain.

AND Gate

Next, let's build an AND gate from NAND and NOT gates. Take a moment before we move forward and see if you can figure out the logical schematic for the AND gate. This is also a very simple gate and we can build its circuit using only half of the 7400 chip. Figure 4.5 shows the logical schematic, and figure 4.6 shows the circuit.

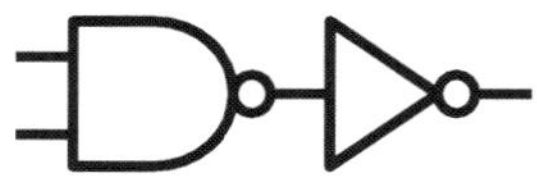

Figure 4.5. Logical AND from NAND and NOT.

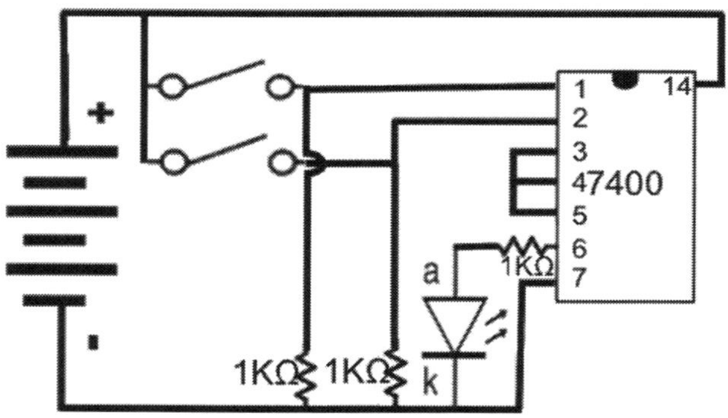

Figure 4.6. AND Circuit Using 7400.

We see in the circuit in Figure 4.6, that we can use two NAND gates from a single 7400 chip. The first gate performs the NAND operation and the second gate performs the NOT function. We use the output from the first gate as both inputs to the second gate. Build this circuit and make sure it works according to the truth table in Figure 4.7.

Input A	Input B	Output
False	False	False
False	True	False
True	False	False
True	True	True

Figure 4.7. AND Truth Table.

OR Gate

Next is a gate that is perhaps a little trickier. It's the OR gate. Figure 4.8 is the truth table for the OR Boolean function.

Input A	Input B	Output
False	False	False
False	True	True
True	False	True
True	True	True

Figure 4.8. OR Truth Table.

Take a minute here to see if you can Figure out how to construct an OR gate using only the gates we have already built. The secret to figuring out this one is to realize that the truth table for the OR looks a lot like an upside down version of an AND. In other words, notice that the only place where an OR has a unique output is when both inputs are false. So the first step is to recognize when both inputs are false. Wanting both inputs to have some condition implies ANDing. And since we want both inputs to be false, we need to invert both inputs.

What we are proposing is running each input through a NOT gate and then ANDing them together. However, the outputs from these three gates in this configuration would be just the opposite of what we want – that is, when both inputs are false, the output would be true, and every other output would be false. When our output is exactly opposite of what we want, it's easy to fix. All we need to do is invert the output. So instead of ANDing the inverted inputs together, we want to NAND the inverted inputs together. Figure 4.9 shows the logic schematic for the OR gate.

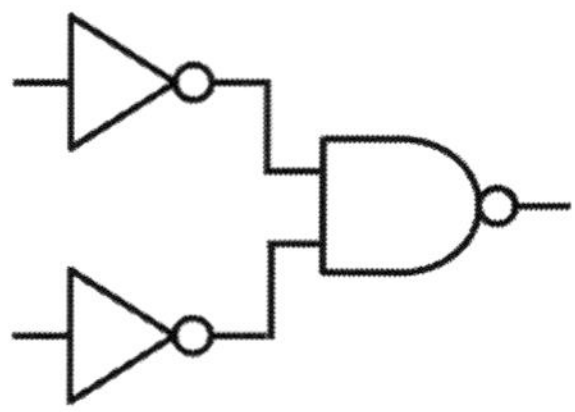

Figure 4.9. Boolean OR from Two NOTs and a NAND.

Notice that you can build the circuit for the schematic in Figure 4.9 with a single 7400 chip and still have an unused NAND gate.

XOR Gate

The final gate we need to build is the XOR gate. This is the most challenging of the gates. Figure 4.10 shows the XOR truth table. Play around a little bit and see if you can figure out how to build this gate.

Input A	Input B	Output
False	False	False
False	True	True
True	False	True
True	True	False

Figure 4.10. XOR Truth Table.

As Boolean functions become more complicated, it becomes more difficult to figure out the logical schematic. One simplifying approach would be to consider building schematics for individual rows of outputs. We only need to consider those outputs that are true. If we can figure out how to build schematics for each of the true output rows, then we can OR these schematics to create the final result.

Let's try this with the XOR table. If we could build a schematic that only outputs true if and only if input A is true and input B is false, and if we can build a second schematic that outputs true only when input A is false and input B is true, then we can take these two outputs and OR them together to create out final schematic.

Each of these two schematics is reasonably simple as shown in Figure 4.11.

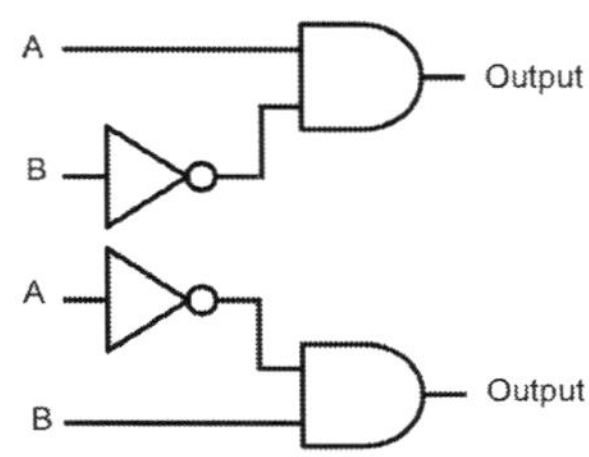

Figure 4.11. Two Schematics for A is True and B is False, and A is False and B is True.

Now we can OR these two schematics together to give us an XOR. We show this in Figure 4.12. Remember, An OR is a NAND with inverted inputs.

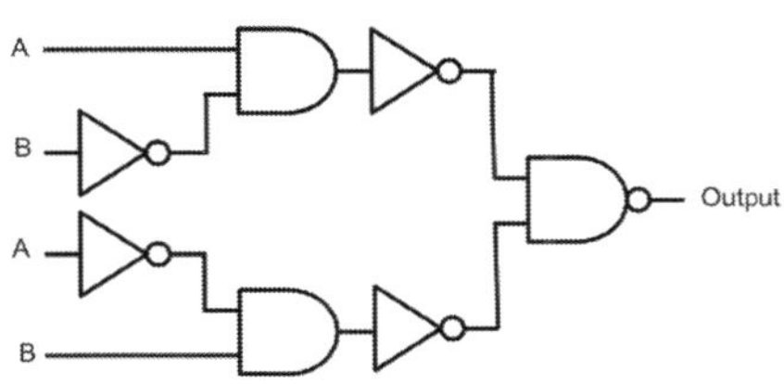

Figure 4.12. Non-optimized XOR Schematic.

The schematic in Figure 4.12 would work well to yield the XOR output. If we think about the implementation of this schematic, we realize it would require nine NAND gates if we simply replaced the Boolean gates with the definitions we previously constructed. Let see if we can optimize this some.

We can represent the schematic in Figure 4.12 as a Boolean expression made up of two sub-expressions:

$$(A \cdot \overline{B}) + (\overline{A} \cdot B)$$

Let's take the left sub-expression first and refactor it. Notice that any Boolean expression OR'd with false is equivalent to the original expression. Further, any Boolean variable AND its NOT is equivalent to false. Therefore, any expression OR a variable AND NOT the same variable is equivalent to the original expression (wow, maybe we need to reread that last sentence). Let's show that with the left sub-expression:

$$(A \cdot \overline{B}) = (A \cdot \overline{B}) + (A \cdot \overline{A})$$

Next we can factor out the A variable. This gives:

$$(A \cdot \overline{B}) = A \cdot (\overline{A} + \overline{B})$$

Finally we can apply De Morgan's law to get:

$$(A \cdot \overline{B}) = A \cdot (\overline{A \cdot B})$$

If we apply this same idea to the right sub-expression, we end up with:

$$(\overline{A} \cdot B) = B \cdot (\overline{A \cdot B})$$

Therefore, by substituting each of these sub-expressions back into the original expression, the entire XOR expression can be rewritten:

$$A \bullet (\overline{A \bullet B}) + B \bullet (\overline{A \bullet B})$$

Now we are ready to redraw the schematic according to this expression as shown in Figure 4.13 (remember what the schematic of OR looks like in Figure 4.9).

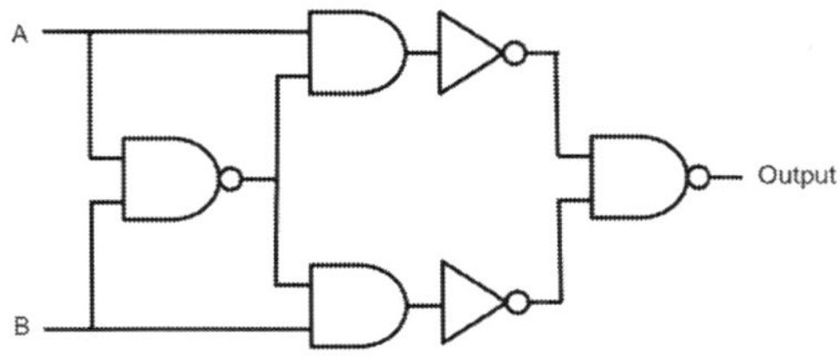

Figure 4.13. XOR with Optimized Inputs.

Finally, rather than using AND gates for the middle two functions and then inverting the output, we can use NAND gates and remove the inverters as shown in Figure 4.14.

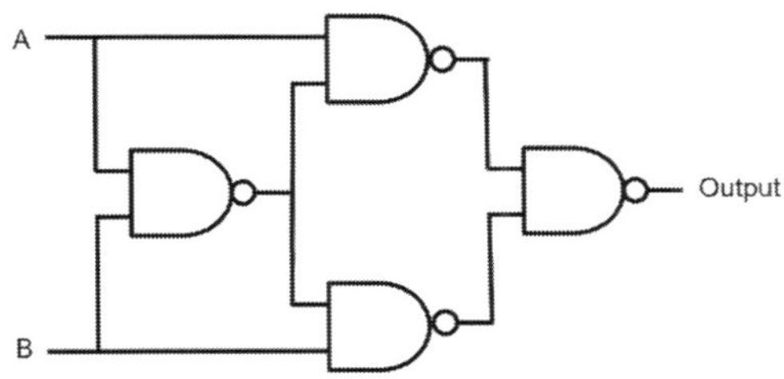

Figure 4.14. Fully Optimized XOR.

As we can see, the schematic in Figure 4.14 only uses four NAND gates – much better than our original nine NAND gates in the non-optimized version. This was a little bit of tricky Boolean algebra, but if we take each step and think carefully, we are able to follow why the schematic in Figure 4.14 is equivalent to the schematic in Figure 4.12. Since it only takes four NAND gates, we can build this circuit with a single 7400 chip. Give it a try and see if it really works.

At this point we have shown that we can create all the basic Boolean functions using only NAND gates. We have moved up three levels of abstraction: from basic electrical circuits, to transistors and finally to Boolean logic gates.

Chip designers also moved up the levels of abstraction. They have created chips that contain gates of each of the basic Boolean functions. Here are the numbers of the various chips:

Boolean Function	Chip Number
NAND	7400
NOT	7404
AND	7408
OR	7432
XOR	7486

In the next chapter we will work with these Boolean functions to move up one more level of abstraction. We will start to build higher-level binary functions from the Boolean logic. Then in later chapters, these higher-level functions will lay the groundwork for building an ALU, a CPU and memory.

Project: Build Each of the Boolean Gates

Let's start by building the circuit described by Figure 4.2. We should experiment with the circuit to satisfy ourselves that it behaves like the NAND gate we constructed using the two transistors.

Next, let's build the NOT gate using a single NAND like the one shown in Figure 4.3. This is straightforward, and helps us become comfortable with a different configuration of the NAND gates.

Now Let's build an AND gate using two NANDs from our 7400 as shown in Figure 4.6. This project helps us see how the output from one NAND can be the input to another.

Also, let's build the circuit for the schematic in Figure 4.9 – the OR gate. Figuring out this schematic is a bit of a logical challenge. Once we understand the logic, the circuit is reasonably simple to build. However, this circuit has more connections, so the possibility of getting something wrong increases. If we have problems with the circuit, we need to carefully trace each of the lines to see what might be misplaced.

Finally, let's build the optimized version of the XOR schematic shown in Figure 4.14. This is the most complex of the schematics. The XOR demonstrates several layers of logical processing.

Hopefully, after building each of these building blocks, we can see how we could build a circuit for any Boolean function of which we could conceive. This is an exciting realization because this means that any function we can express in terms of a Boolean expression, we can build a circuit to model it. This realization is the key idea behind electronic computation.

For the circuits in this chapter you will need the following:

- 1 breadboard
- 1 power source (either a wall wart or a battery supply pack)
- 2 pushbutton switches
- 1 LED
- 1 1KΩ resistor
- 6 jumper wires
- 1 7400 chip

We use basic Boolean functions to create higher-level binary functions. We will build adders, multi-bit Boolean functions, shifters, multiplexors and demultiplexors. We then combine all of these binary components into an ALU. The ALU is at the heart of digital electronic computation.

Chapter 5 – Arithmetic Logic Unit

We have covered a lot of ground so far in our journey to understand computer architecture. Let's reflect about where we have come from. We started out with a simple electronic circuit and learned some of the basic principles of electronics. We proceeded to understand the role of transistors in digital electronics. We used transistors to build NAND gates, which are the fundamental building blocks of all digital logic. Finally, we used the NAND gates to build all of the foundational Boolean functions.

In this chapter we will move from our Boolean world into a binary world. We will use the Boolean function we constructed in the previous chapter to create binary functions that start to look like recognizable computing constructs. These constructs make up the Arithmetic Logic Unit (ALU).

Let's start by identifying the capabilities of the ALU. The ALU performs a subset of the processor's functionality that deals with math operations and logic. Specifically the math operations include addition and subtraction. The logical operations include mainly AND, OR and NOT. We can also add one additional useful operation known as shifting, which moves the position of each bit to the side.

We have already looked at the Boolean logical operations of gates. What's the difference between gate-level Boolean operations and ALU Boolean operations? There are two differences. First, we think of gate-level operations as operating on Boolean values, but as we move to the ALU, we think of these operations as working on binary numbers. Really, it's the same circuitry, but we view it differently.

The second difference at the ALU level is that we scale these operations to work in parallel so that we can perform the Boolean operations on many bits, an entire binary number, at once. In order to accomplish this parallel scaling we will introduce some additional control circuitry made from the Boolean gates we establish in the previous chapter.

The size of the parallel scaling depends on the word size. A word consists of an ordered set of bits used as a standard parameter in the operations of a processor. The number of bits in the set constitutes the word size. Normally, word sizes are powers of two, for reasons that will become apparent as we work through the design. The choice of the size is somewhat arbitrary. We want enough bits to represent numbers of a useful size, but increasing the number of bits also adds to the cost of the design, so we want to keep the number of bits small to reduce cost. These counteracting forces cause designers to choose word sizes of 16, 32 or 64 bits. Since we are more interested in exploring design rather than building a world-class processor, we will use a 16-bit word.

Adders

Before we try to build all the ALU functions at scale, let's understand how the individual functions of the ALU work. We have already looked at the AND and OR functionality at the gate level which we can directly apply at the bit level. Let's now take a look at addition.

Let's start by creating a circuit for adding two bits together. We call this a one-bit adder – yes, we are adding two bits together, but the main output is a single bit, hence, one-bit adder. First let's look at the truth table for this function as shown in Table 5.1. Note that this table is no longer Boolean. Instead it's Binary.

Bit A	Bit B	CarryOut	Output
0	0	0	0
0	1	0	1
1	0	0	1
1	1	1	0

Figure 5.1. One-Bit Adder Truth Table.

Even though the table in Figure 5.1 is binary, we can treat the values in a way similar to Boolean by considering zero to be false, and one to be true. Another interesting aspect of this table is that it has two outputs – one labeled *CarryOut*, and the other labeled *Output*. These two outputs work together to represent a two-bit binary number. The Output is the low-order bit. The CarryOut is the high-order bit. These two bits are necessary when both inputs are ones as shown in the last row of the truth table. We will explain later why we refer to the high-order bit as CarryOut.

The easiest way to conceptualize this function is to see each output as it's own function. By doing this, we see that the Output function is merely an XOR, and the CarryOut function is just an AND. Figure 5.2 shows the schematic for a one-bit adder.

Figure 5.2. One-bit Adder Schematic.

There are two key points about the schematic in Figure 5.1. First, we moved from Boolean to binary. Second, we isolated each output to simplify the design effort.

While adding two bits is a step towards computation, it would be much more interesting to understand how to add more than two bits. For example, imagine adding two-bit values. Figure 5.3 shows the truth table for this adder.

Input A2	Input A1	Input B2	Input B1	CarryOut	Output 2	Output 1
0	0	0	0	0	0	0
0	0	0	1	0	0	1
0	0	1	0	0	1	0
0	0	1	1	0	1	1
0	1	0	0	0	0	1
0	1	0	1	0	1	0
0	1	1	0	0	1	1
0	1	1	1	1	0	0
1	0	0	0	0	1	0
1	0	0	1	0	1	1
1	0	1	0	1	0	0
1	0	1	1	1	0	1
1	1	0	0	0	1	1
1	1	0	1	1	0	0
1	1	1	0	1	0	1
1	1	1	1	1	1	0

Figure 5.3. Two-bit Adder Truth Table.

This is a function with four inputs and three outputs. Further, the four inputs are really two sets of two inputs each. Each set of two has a high-order bit (representing the twos place) and a low-order bit (representing the ones place). The three output bits represent the fours place (CarryOut), the twos place and the ones place respectively.

Once again, an easy way to approach the schematic design of the entire function is to design the schematic for each individual output, and then combine the schematics. Taking this approach, we see that the two low-order bits behave in the same manner as the single one-bit adder shown in Figure 5.2. That is to say, that Output 1 for the two-bit adder is the same as the Output for the one-bit adder, but, what about the CarryOut from the one-bit adder in Figure 5.2?

The CarryOut from the low-order bits becomes an input (call it CarryIn) along with inputs A2 and B2 for Output 2. The table in Figure 5.3 shows the dependencies between these three inputs and the output.

Input A2	Input B2	CarryIn	Output 2
0	0	0	0
0	0	1	1
0	1	0	1
0	1	1	0
1	0	0	1
1	0	1	0
1	1	0	0
1	1	1	1

Figure 5.3. Output 2 Truth Table.

The function in Figure 5.3 is a three-way XOR, or in other words, and XOR of A2 and B2 where the output is the input to and XOR with the CarryIn.

Finally, we need to look at the third output in Figure 5.3 labeled CarryOut, which is also a function of the A2 and B2 inputs as well as the CarryIn. Let's look at its isolated truth table as shown in Figure 5.4.

Input A2	Input B2	CarryIn	CarryOut
0	0	0	0
0	0	1	0
0	1	0	0
0	1	1	1
1	0	0	0
1	0	1	1
1	1	0	1
1	1	1	1

Figure 5.4. CarryOut Truth Table.

This is not an obvious function. We need a different way to think about this strange function.

Karnaugh Maps

From time-to-time when doing logic design, we run into digital functions that seem to be strange and we need to figure out the circuitry. In 1953, Maurice Karnaugh came up with a way to do just that using something known as Karnaugh maps, or K-maps. The explanation for how Karnaugh maps work is a little confusing, but we mustn't let that scare us off. Once we understand how they work, they are really pretty simple and very helpful.

Karnaugh maps work by creating a table a bit like our truth tables. We can then use these tables to help us identify the algebraic formula that represents the function. Given the algebraic formula, it becomes relatively easy to convert the formula into a schematic. Let's work through some examples, and then we will apply Karnaugh maps to figure out what the strange function is for CarryOut in Figure 5.4.

For our first example, let's imagine we have a simple function with two inputs, but we aren't sure what the function is. The function might have a truth table like that shown in Figure 5.5.

Input A	Input B	Output
0	0	1
0	1	1
1	0	1
1	1	0

Figure 5.5. A Simple Mystery Function Truth Table.

In order to figure out the algebraic formula for this function, we construct a Karnaugh map. Karnaugh maps are always two-dimensional tables. These tables represent some of the inputs of the function along the vertical axis, and the other inputs along the horizontal axis. Figure 5.6 shows a Karnaugh map for our mystery function.

A\B	0	1
0	1	1
1	1	0

Figure 5.6. A Karnaugh Map for the Mystery Function.

The top-left cell of the Karnaugh map in Figure 5.6 is a label that tells us that the far left column represents the input A, and the top row represents the input B. The shaded cells of the map represent inputs to the function. The non-shaded cells of the map represent the outputs for the combinations of the inputs. So, for example, the cell in the middle of the map represents the result when input A is 0 and input B is 0. The cell on the far right of the middle row represents the output given input A is 0 and input B is 1. The cell in the center of the bottom row represents the output when input A is 1 and input

B is 0. Finally, the cell in the bottom-right represents the output when both inputs A and B are 1.

Next, we look at the pattern of 1's in the output area of the map. To find a pattern, we want to circle as many contiguous 1's that are in a matrix formation, such that the dimensions of the formed matrix are a power of two. The previous sentence may seem a little hard to digest, but follow these examples and you will get the hang of it. For the map in Figure 5.6, we will circle the output cells in the middle row (where A = 0), and also circle the center column (where B = 0). Figure 5.7 shows the result.

A\B	0	1
0	1	1
1	1	0

Figure 5.7. Karnaugh Map with Circled Patterns.

Now we look at each of the patterns we have circled and we describe the patterns in terms of their inputs. In this example, we have two patterns, a horizontal circle and a vertical circle. We can describe the horizontal circle as NOT A, since A is 0 for all values in the circle. Similarly, we can describe the vertical circle as NOT B. To complete the algebraic formula, we OR the two patterns together to form NOT A OR NOT B.

$$\overline{A} + \overline{B}$$

Notice that we can refactor this expression by using De Morgan's law to get A NAND B, which becomes very easy to convert into a Schematic.

$$\overline{A \cdot B}$$

Let's look at a little more complex function. Consider the truth table in Figure 5.8.

A	B	C	Output
0	0	0	0
0	0	1	1
0	1	0	0
0	1	1	0
1	0	0	0
1	0	1	1
1	1	0	1
1	1	1	1

Figure 5.8. Three Input Mystery Function.

This function seems to have no discernable pattern, so let's apply a Karnaugh map to it. Remember that Karnaugh maps are two-dimensional. So, how do we create a two-dimensional map when we have three dimensions of input? Well, one of the dimensions of the map needs to represent more than one input. Figure 5.9 shows the Karnaugh map. We use the vertical dimension to represent the A and B inputs.

AB\C	0	1
00	0	1
01	0	0
11	1	1
10	0	1

Figure 5.9. Three Input Mystery Function Karnaugh Map.

Notice that the Vertical dimension axis represents the value of the A and B inputs while the horizontal axis represents the C input. Also, it is important to note that the order of the A and B inputs on the vertical axis is significant. The value of the A and B inputs must only change by one bit from one row to the next. Hence, the two inputs do not follow a normal binary counting sequence (i.e., 11 follows 01 instead of 10 following 01).

Next, we need to circle the patterns of ones. Remember that we want to circle as many contiguous 1's as we can such that the number of rows and the number of columns of the circled pattern is a power of two. As we circle the patterns of ones on this Karnaugh map, we will illustrate two things to keep in mind.

First, the patterns can wrap around the map. In this example, the cell in the top-right may be combined with the cell in the bottom-right. But we cannot combine the cell for the input value 111 into the pattern with the other cells on the right because that would not create a pattern with height that is a power of two. However, we can create a second pattern that would consist of the cells based on the inputs 110 and 111.

Second, we only need to create enough patterns to cover all the output 1's. In the example, we could create a third pattern based on the inputs 111 and 101. Although it's OK if patterns overlap, in this case we do not need to create this pattern because the other two patterns already cover all of these cells. Figure 5.10 shows the circling of the patterns we will use to create the schematic for this function.

AB\C	0	1
00	0	1
01	0	0
11	1	1
10	0	1

Figure 5.10. Three Input Mystery Function Karnaugh Map with Circled Patterns.

To derive the algebraic expression, we look at what inputs remain constant for each of the patterns. This yields the following:

$$(A \cdot B) + (\overline{B} \cdot C)$$

Just to be clear, this expression maps directly to the schematic in Figure 5.11.

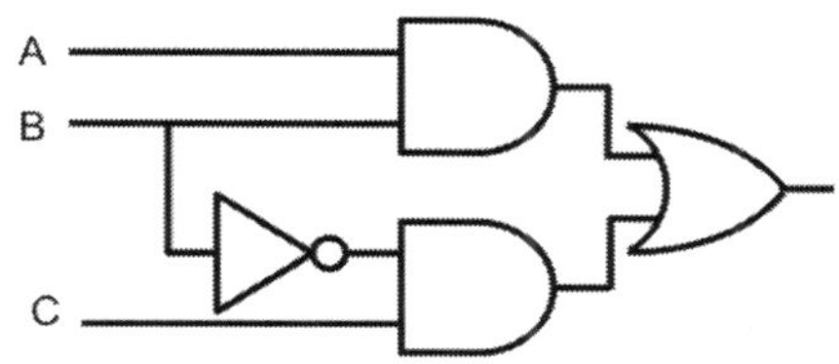

Figure 5.11. Schematic for Three Input Mystery Function.

Now let's return to the strange CarryOut function depicted in Figure 5.4 and see if we can apply the Karnaugh map. Figure 5.12 shows a Karnaugh map for the function described in Figure 5.4.

A2B2\CarryIn	0	1
00	0	0
01	0	1
11	1	1
10	0	1

Figure 5.12. The Karnaugh Map for the Carry Column.

This map has three expressions that result in the following:

$$(A2 \cdot B2) + (B2 \cdot Carry) + (A2 \cdot Carry)$$

We see that we can refactor this expression to:

$$(A2 \cdot B2) + (Carry \cdot (A2 + B2))$$

We can convert this expression into a logical schematic – but not so fast. We can do a bit of an optimization and take advantage of some previous work.

Recall that the schematic for the Output 2 column is an XOR function for inputs A2 and B2. Is it possible that we could use this calculation to calculate the new Carry output? This optimization is not immediately obvious, but people have been working on adders long enough that they have discovered this reuse of the XOR function. Here's how it works in proof format:

$$
\begin{aligned}
&(A2 \cdot B2) + (Carry \cdot (A2 + B2)) \\
&\quad = (A2 \cdot B2) + (Carry \cdot ((A2 + \overline{A2}) \cdot (A2 + B2))) \\
&\quad = (A2 \cdot B2) + (Carry \cdot (A2 + (\overline{A2} \cdot B2))) \\
&\quad = (A2 \cdot B2) + (Carry \cdot ((A2 \cdot B2) + (A2 \cdot \overline{B2}) + (\overline{A2} \cdot B2))) \\
&\quad = (A2 \cdot B2) + (A2 \cdot B2 \cdot Carry) + (A2 \cdot \overline{B2} \cdot Carry) + \\
&\qquad\qquad (\overline{A2} \cdot B2 \cdot Carry) \\
&\quad = ((A2 \cdot B2) + Carry) \cdot ((A2 \cdot B2) + (A2 \cdot \overline{B2}) + (\overline{A2} \cdot B2)) \\
&\quad = ((A2 \cdot B2) + Carry) \cdot ((A2 \cdot B2) + (A2 \oplus B2)) \\
&\quad = (A2 \cdot B2) + (Carry) \cdot (A2 \oplus B2))
\end{aligned}
$$

If the algebraic proof is a little hard to follow, it may be helpful to consider the Venn diagram in Figure 5.13.

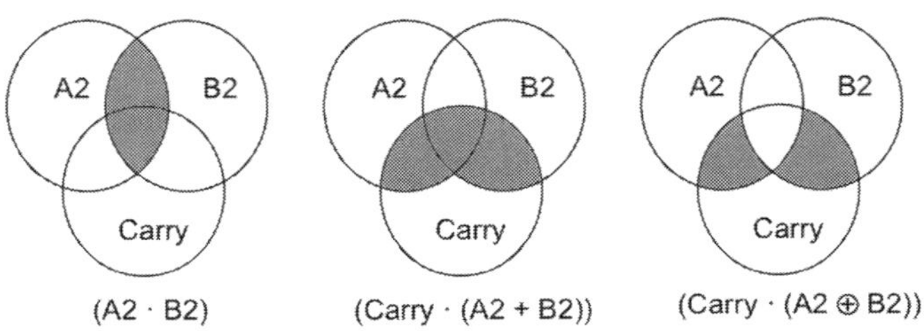

Figure 5.13. Venn Diagram Representing the Terms of the Proof.

The three diagrams in Figure 5.13 represent the separate terms of the proof. The left most term represents (A2 • B2), which is common in both the starting expression and the ending expression of the proof. The center diagram represents (Carry • (A2 + B2)), which, when combined with the left diagram, covers the area between A2, B2 and Carry. Similarly, the right most diagram, which represents (Carry • (A2 ⊕ B2)), when combined with the left most diagram covers the area between A2, B2 and Carry. Therefore the expressions are equivalent.

We can reduce this resultant expression to a schematic as shown in Figure 5.14.

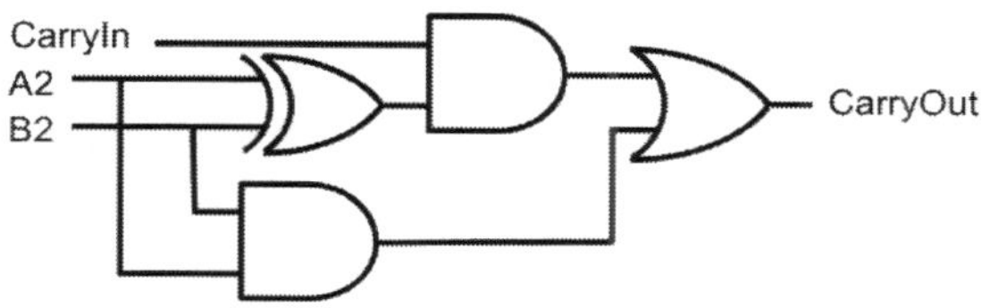

Figure 5.14. Carry Column Schematic.

To complete the two-bit adder, we could combine all of the three output column schematics as shown in figure 5.15.

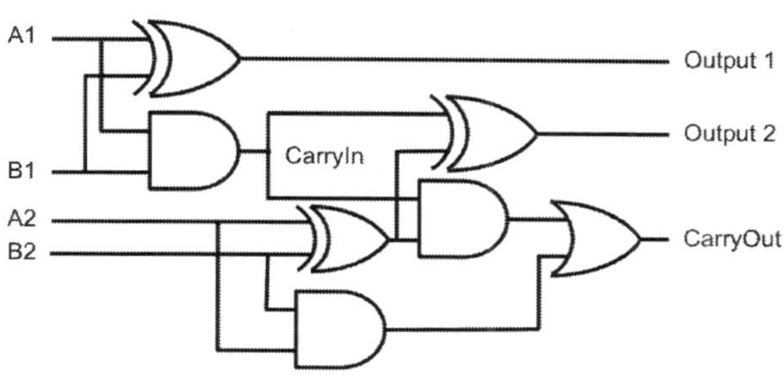

Figure 5.15. Two-bit Adder Schematic.

Rippling Adders

At this point, let's reflect on our next step. In order to create a three-bit adder, we could go through the same work to figure out the functions, etc., or we can make the observation that adding the third bit is a lot like the second bit. In other words, the third bit will require two bits as input, call them A3 and B3, as well as a carry from the addition of bits A2 and B2. The schematic for adding two bits is the same for all but the first two bits. The reason the schematic is different for adding the first two bits is because the first two bits have no carry input.

Another way to look at it is that the CarryIn, when adding the first two bits, is zero. If we think about adding the first two bits with a CarryIn of zero, then we realize that we are able to generalize the adder we have designed for adding bits A2 and B2, to adding any two bits we want. This general one-bit adder looks like the schematic in Figure 5.16.

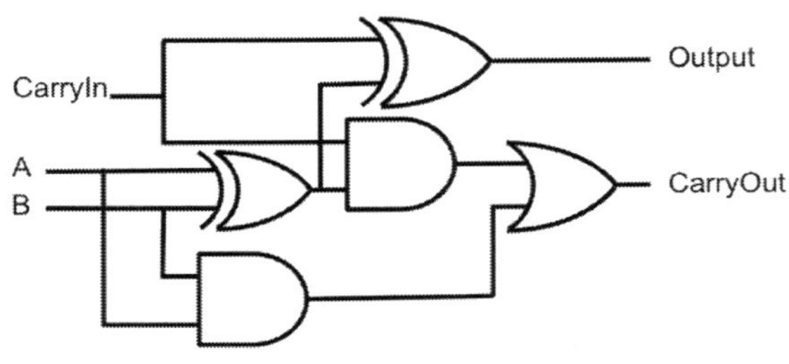

Figure 5.16. Generalized One-bit Adder Schematic.

Now, given a generalized one-bit adder, we can connect many of these together to add two or more bits. To show how this is done, let's move up one level of abstraction like we did when we moved from transistors to NANDs, or like when we moved from NANDs to general Boolean gates. We can represent the generalized one-bit adder with a single box like that shown in Figure 5.17.

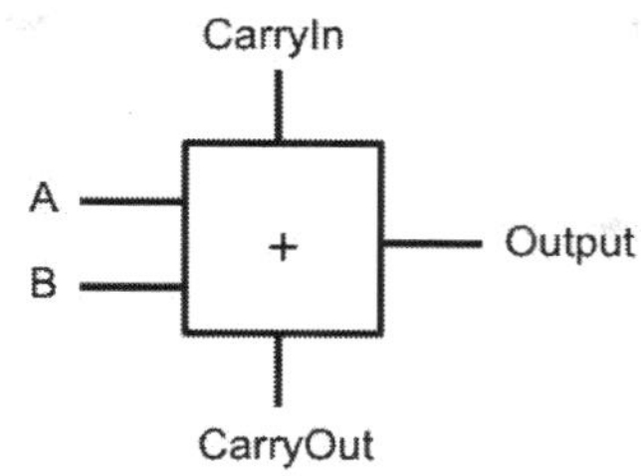

Figure 5.17. Generalize One-bit Adder Symbol.

The symbol in Figure 5.17 is equivalent to the schematic in figure 5.16. We can connect these generalized adders together to create a ripple adder. Figure 5.18 shows a four-bit ripple adder. Remember, we set the CarryIn to zero for the first adder in the ripple, but each subsequent adder gets its CarryIn value from the previous adder in the ripple.

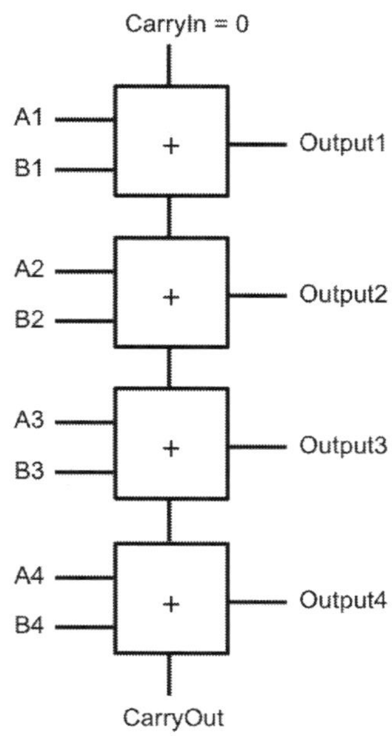

Figure 5.18. Four-bit Ripple Adder Schematic.

Once we have an adder, it is quite straightforward to create subtraction. The secret to understanding subtraction has two steps. The first step is to understand that subtraction really means just adding a negative. For example, the expression X-Y is really the same thing as X+(-Y). The second step is to remember how to get the negative of a number using twos-complement binary. Using twos-complement binary, we get the negative by inverting all the bits of a positive binary number, and then add one (-X = NOT(X)+1). We get NOT(X) by inverting each of the bits with a NOT gate, and we add one by setting the CarryIn on the first adder to 1. Figure 5.19 shows four-bit subtraction.

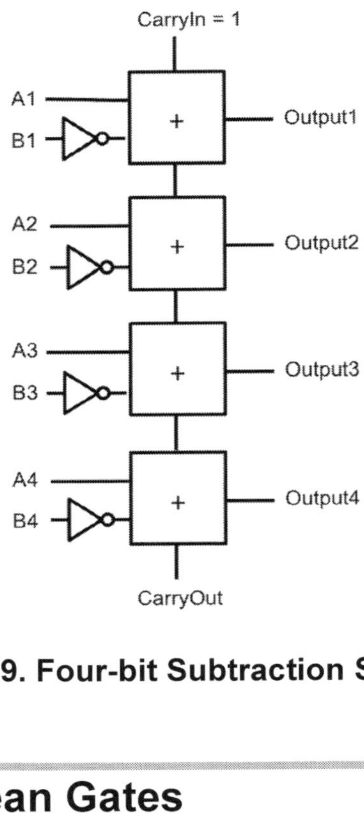

Figure 5.19. Four-bit Subtraction Schematic.

N-Way Boolean Gates

As we mentioned earlier, the ALU functionality will also include the AND operator. We can scale AND in a manner similar to the way we scaled addition and subtraction. Figure 5.20

shows the schematic for a scaled four-bit binary AND function. Obviously, we could scale OR the same way.

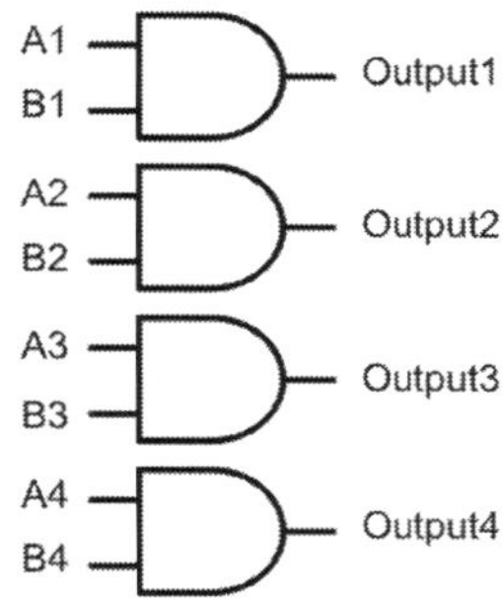

Figure 5.20. Four-bit AND.

Multiplexors and Demultiplexors

We have shown how to create the four main functions of the ALU: add, subtract, AND and OR. Next we need to figure out how to select one of these functions. The main idea here is that we will calculate the result for each of the four functions in parallel, and then decide which operation we are interested in. The way we would perform the operations in parallel would be as easy as presenting the same inputs to each of the four functions (i.e., add, subtract, AND and OR). But determining which of the four outputs to use requires a figuring out another building block circuit called a *multiplexor*.

The idea behind a multiplexor is that I have binary inputs to choose from, a single binary output, and a selection pattern. A black box schematic description might look like Figure 5.21.

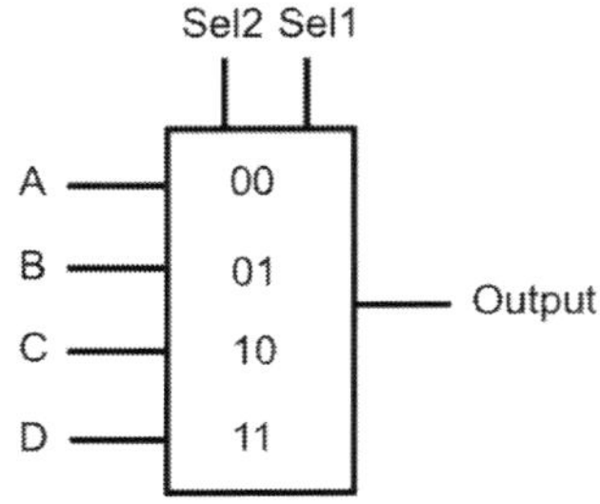

Figure 5.21. Multiplexor Black Box Schematic.

The multiplexor in Figure 5.21 works in a way such that the values of Sel2 and Sel1 determine the output. Figure 5.22 is a truth table for the multiplexor in Figure 5.21.

Sel2	Sel1	Output
0	0	A
0	1	B
1	0	C
1	1	D

Figure 5.22. Multiplexor Truth Table.

The logic for the multiplexor works by ANDing various combinations of Sel2 and Sel1 with each of the four binary inputs and then ORing all the results together. The Boolean expression for the multiplexor looks like:

$$(\overline{\text{Sel2}} \bullet \overline{\text{Sel1}} \bullet \text{A}) + (\overline{\text{Sel2}} \bullet \text{Sel1} \bullet \text{B}) +$$
$$(\text{Sel2} \bullet \overline{\text{Sel1}} \bullet \text{C}) + (\text{Sel2} \bullet \text{Sel1} \bullet \text{D})$$

We can build a three-way AND by taking the results of a two-way AND and ANDing the result with the third input. Similarly, we can build a four-way OR with the results of two ORs ORed together. Figure 5.23 shows the schematic for a multiplexor equivalent to the expression.

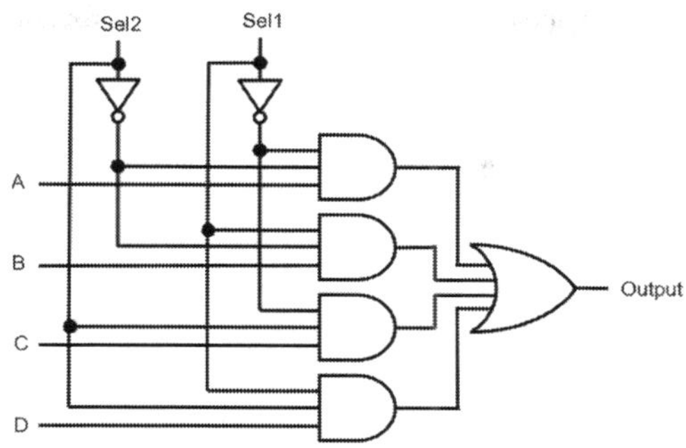

Figure 5.23. Multiplexor Schematic.

We can also refactor the expression for the multiplexor so that the expression only uses two-way ANDs and ORs as follows:

$$(\overline{Sel2} \bullet ((Sel1 \bullet A) + (\overline{Sel1} \bullet B))) +$$

$$(Sel2 \bullet ((\overline{Sel1} \bullet C) + (Sel1 \bullet D)))$$

Given this refactored expression, we can see that our four-input multiplexor is really just two two-input multiplexors that we combine into a third two-input multiplexor. Figure 5.24 shows the schematic for this refactored multiplexor.

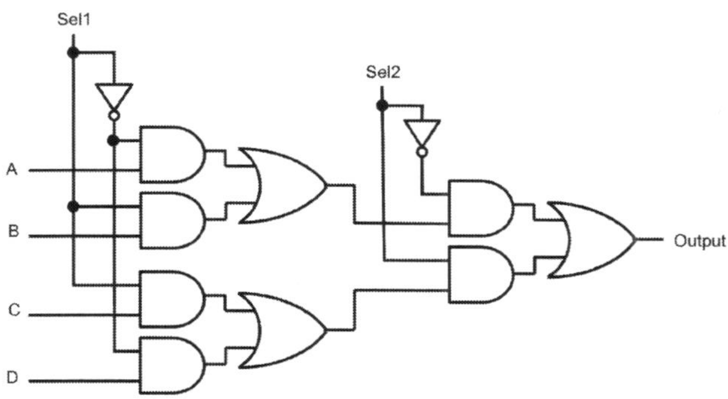

Figure 5.24. The Refactored Multiplexor.

It is important to see the pattern in this refactored multiplexor so that we know how to build multiplexors of any size by cascading them together. For example, we could create an eight-input multiplexor by taking the outputs from two four-input multiplexors and using these outputs as inputs to yet another two-input multiplexor.

As we can see the purpose of the multiplexor is to produce one output from several inputs. We can imagine it would also be helpful to do the opposite – to produce one of several outputs from a single input. This is called a *demultiplexor*. Figure 5.25 shows the schematic for a two-by-four demultiplexor.

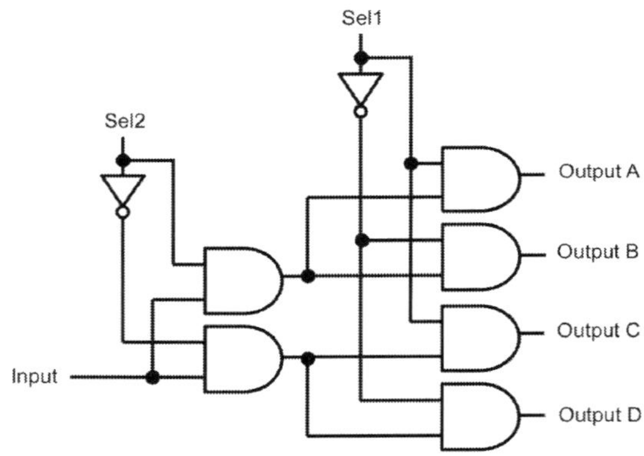

Figure 5.25. Two-by-four Demultiplexor Schematic.

We can see from Figure 5.25 that we can also cascade demultiplexors so that we can build larger demultiplexors from the simple one-by-two demultiplexors. As a result, we can design easily demultiplexors of any size.

Let's think back to the adder. We can use a simple multiplexor to turn-on the invertor for the B input of the adder. Of course, we will have to replicate this invertor for each of the B inputs to the adder, but all of these simple multiplexors can share the same select line. Additionally, we can use the same select line as the CarryIn to the adder. This has the effect of being able to select between addition and subtraction by merely toggling the select line.

Shifters

We can use this simple multiplexor in another useful way. We can connect a series of these simple multiplexors so that the result is the input shifted by one or more positions. Figure 5.26 shows the schematic for a shifter that can shift bits either zero or one position.

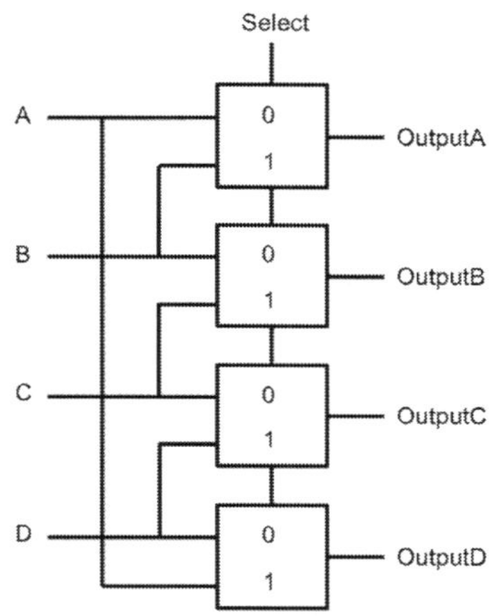

Figure 5.26. One Position Shift (Rotate).

In Figure 5.26, all the Select lines are connected. When Select is 0, the output matches the input. When Select is 1, OutputA is B, OutputB is C, etc. Notice also that when Select is 1, OutputD is A which causes a rotation from one end to the other.

We can take the output of this shifter and use it as the input to another shifter. This configuration would allow us to rotate zero, one or two positions. However, if we cause the second shifter to move two positions instead of one, the resulting schematic allows for rotation of zero, one, two or three positions, depending on the select lines settings.

We can play this game another time by taking the output of the second shifter and running it into a third shifter. This would allow us to rotate up to seven positions. Since, in our example, we only have four inputs, it doesn't make sense to shift more than three times, but with a larger word size, it would make sense. Figure 5.27 shows a shifter that allows rotating from zero to three positions. This is known as a barrel shifter.

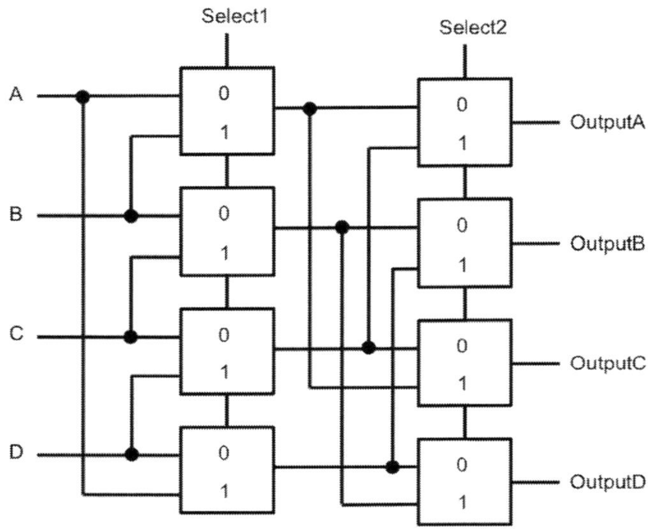

Figure 5.27. Four-bit Barrel Shifter.

In the previous ALU functions we have had two inputs. The barrel shifter appears to have only one input, but we can use the second input to indicate how many places to shift the input.

ALU

We have now created the four main ALU functions. These main functions are add, AND, OR and shift.

How do we tell the ALU which function to perform? We will use a two-by-four multiplexor to combine the outputs from the four main ALU functions. In this way, each of the functions computes its outputs in parallel, and then the multiplexor decides which output to use. This gives us the equivalent of being able to choose any of the main functions, as well as their variations, by toggling the selection lines on the invertor and the four-way multiplexor.

Notice also that all of the functions share the same input, but if we connect the logical functions' (i.e., AND and OR) inputs just after the invertors we can get some additional functionality. Once we realize this, we can see that it makes sense to be able to invert either the A or the B input. By adding this second invertor on the A input, we achieve the NOR functionality. How do we get NOR? If we invert both inputs to the AND function, we can achieve NOR because of De Morgan's Law. In fact, this second invertor gives us lots of flexibility in the functions we can realize. Figure 5.28 shows the schematic for the full four-bit ALU.

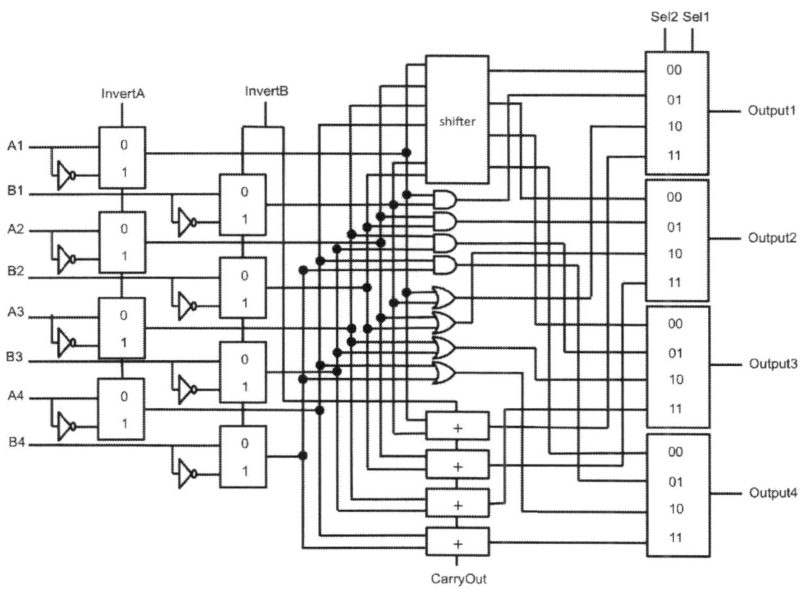

Figure 5.28. Full four-bit ALU Schematic.

At first glance, this ALU schematic in Figure 5.28 may seem a bit overwhelming, but with just a little bit of study we should be able to make sense of it. We have already become familiar with all of its subcomponents, so understanding the ALU is just a matter of seeing how the subcomponents connect together.

We see from the four-bit ALU schematic in Figure 5.28, that the ALU has eight inputs (four for the A input and four for the B input). We see also that the ALU has four control lines: two for inverting A and B, and two for selecting one of the four functions (shift, AND, OR or addition/subtraction). Setting the Select lines to 00 gives shift results, 01 gives AND results, 10 gives OR results and 11 gives addition/subtraction results. The results of these functions show up on the four ALU output lines on the right.

On the left side of the schematic, we see that all inputs for both A and B can be inverted using InvertA and InvertB. This schematic also shows how the ALU uses the InvertB line to affect the CarryIn line of the first adder, which together with the invertor gives the subtraction functionality. If we trace the lines coming out of the invertor section, we see that the ALU connects all the inputs to all of the ALU's functions.

The middle section of the schematic shows each of the four ALU functions. From top to bottom, these are shift, AND, OR and addition/subtraction. The right side of the ALU uses multiplexors to determine which of the functions outputs to use as the final output of the ALU.

While this is a 4-bit ALU, it is pretty easy to see how we could scale this design to 8, 16 or even 32 bits just be replicating the logic we have already created.

One more minor note; in this ALU, we are not determining overflow during the addition/subtraction operation. Overflow is different than carry. Overflow is reasonably easy to detect by looking at the last adder. When the CarryIn is different than the CarryOut on the last adder, we have overflow. It would be easy enough to tap into these two lines (i.e., CarryIn and CarryOut of the last adder), and XOR these lines. The result of the XOR would be another output from the ALU.

This chapter has been quite a journey! We have moved beyond simple Boolean functions to binary, and have extended the binary functions to a full-fledged ALU. In the next chapter we will start to look at some of the other functions necessary to build a complete CPU.

Project: Build an ALU

For this project we won't use actual hardware. Instead we can use a hardware simulator – Logisim. Logisim is a great open-source project, written by Dr. Carl Burch, which allows us to create projects just like having a breadboard. We can download Logisim from:

http://www.cburch.com/logisim/download.html.

We can also find tutorials at the same site to help us learn how to use Logisim, but don't worry. Logisim is easy to use and very intuitive.

Start by building a one-bit adder from Boolean gates. Play with the adder so that you understand how it works including it inputs, output and carry.

Once we understand how to build an adder, we can use the adder provided by Logisim. We could easily configure the Logisim adder to add 16-bits, but let's create our own out of 16 one-bit adders to show that we understand how to ripple the adders.

Notice how Logisim allows us to create our own modules similar to the way we created the adder module in this chapter. These modules behave like black boxes where we can define the inputs and the outputs.

Next, let's try creating a 16-bit AND and a 16-bit OR. Once again, we could just configure Logisim to do the AND and OR for us, but right now let's build them from two-bit ANDs and ORs.

Try building a two-by-four multiplexor and a two-by-four demultiplexor. These will have two control lines and four data lines. Once we demonstrate we understand how to build these, we can just use the built-in Logisim versions. But building it ourselves first will cement our understanding.

We can build a 16-shifter as described in this chapter. We can build this shifter using the built-in Logisim multiplexors. The main point of this project is to show we understand how to wire up the multiplexors.

Finally, we can use all of these parts to build a fully functional ALU. The ALU should have two 16-bit data inputs, two inverter control lines, two operation control lines and one 16-bit data output line. If we want to get fancy, our ALU could also have an overflow output line.

This project will be a little more work than previous projects, but when we are done, we will have a huge part of the CPU – the ALU. It is a blast to start to see this come together, so even though this will take a little bit more effort, we will be surprised at how fast the time will fly as we work on this project!

This chapter looks at circuits with a feedback loop. We use these circuits for things like memory, clocks and timers. These sequential circuits are the missing pieces we need before we are ready to build a complete computer.

Chapter 6 – Sequential Circuits

So far, every circuit we have designed has been deterministic in the sense that if we know the current inputs, we can determine the outputs. However, to build a computer, we need to be able to do more than this. We sometimes need to save the output from a circuit so we can refer back to it later.

Bits, Registers and Memory

In order to remember an output, we will need more sophisticated circuits than we have seen to this point. We can build these circuits out of the same simple Boolean gates, just like our previous circuits, but we need to add one new concept: *feedback*. Feedback is when we take the output from some function, process or circuit and use it as an input to that same function, process or circuit.

For example, we could build a circuit like the one in Figure 6.1 known as a *latch* circuit. At first blush, this circuit seems simple enough. We made the circuit out of two NAND gates. We connected each of the NAND gates' outputs to the other NAND gates' inputs. What on earth does this circuit do?

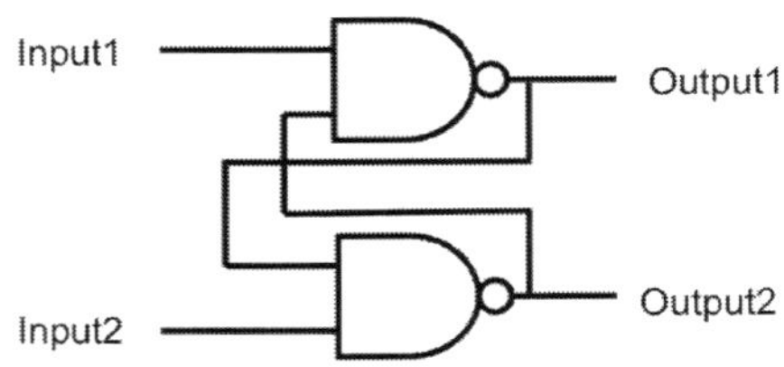

Figure 6.1. Latch Circuit.

Let's reason about this circuit for a minute. If we set both inputs to 0, we know that both outputs will be 1. How do we know this? Because by definition when we NAND anything with 0 the result is 1. Next, if we set Input1 to 0, but we change Input2 is 1, then Output1 will be 1 (because if we NAND anything with 0 we get 1), but Output2 changes to 0 (because both inputs to the lower NAND are 1). Conversely, if we had changed Input1 to 1 and had left Input2 as 0, Output1 would have changed to 0 and Output2 would remain 1. It's worth building this circuit and trying the various inputs until we feel comfortable with how the latch works.

The strange part about the Latch circuit is that if both inputs are 1, we can't really determine the outputs without knowing the prior state of the latch. Therefore, let's be careful when we let the latch have both inputs as 1. How can we do this? First, let's synchronize both inputs so that they happen at the same time, then we can put in some logic to make sure the inputs are always opposite. We will use NANDs to do this since they are the fundamental building block for digital logic. Figure 6.2 shows a circuit that synchronizes the inputs to the latch.

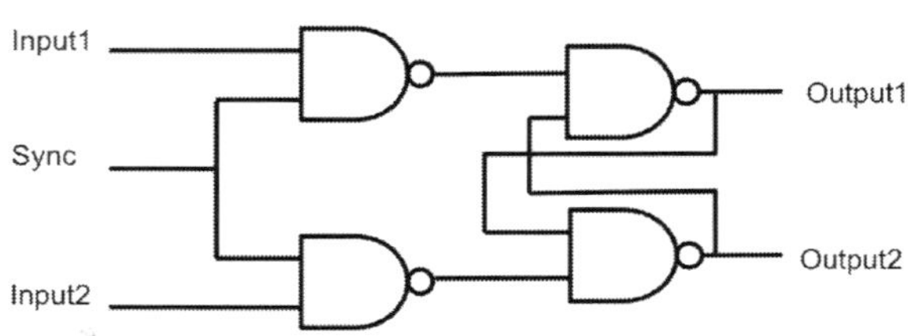

Figure 6.2. Latch with Synchronized Inputs.

With the synchronized latch shown in Figure 6.2, we can set the Sync input to 0 until we have the other inputs ready. Then we can pulse the Sync input by momentarily setting Sync to 1 and then returning Sync back to 0. While we could try all four of the possible combinations of values for Input1 and Input2, we are really interested in only those values that are opposite, i.e., when Input1 is 1 and Input2 is 0, or when Input1 is 0 and Input2 is 1. Notice that when we set these values accordingly and pulse the Sync input, the latch's outputs maintain the values of their inputs. So, for example, if Input1 is 0 and Input2 is 1, when we pulse Sync, Output1 becomes 0 and Output2 becomes1. It is also worthwhile to build this circuit and play with it until we are comfortable with its operation – focusing on opposing input values.

Since we are only focusing on opposing input values, it seems a bit silly to have to input both values when we can logically derive the value of the second input from the first by adding an inverter. We can use a NAND gate for the invertor just to show that we can construct the entire circuit from NAND gates. We call this circuit a *flip-flop* as Figure 6.3 shows. There are various kinds of flip-flop circuits. This one is known as a D-type flip-flop.

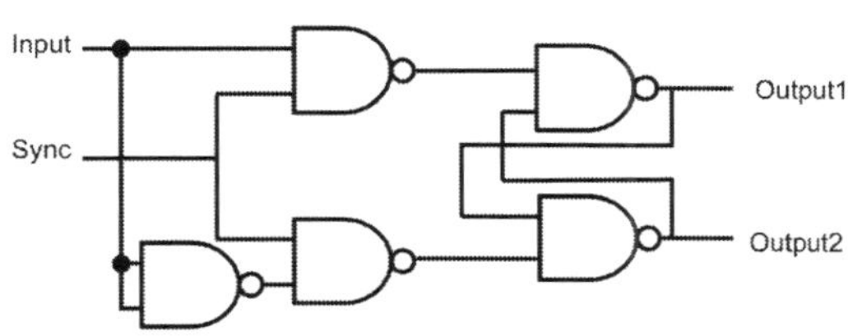

Figure 6.3. D-Type Flip-flop Circuit.

Here are some points of interest about the flip-flop circuit shown in Figure 6.3. First we notice that we only need one input. What used to be the second input is now derived by inverting the input. When we build this circuit and play with it, we notice that Output1 follows Input1. In other words, if Input1 is 0 when we pulse Sync, then Output1 will be 0. Similarly, if

Input1 is 1 when we pulse Sync, then Output1 will be 1. We also notice that Output2 is the inverse of Output1. We can use Output2 if we ever need the inverse of Output1.

We can draw a box around the circuit in Figure 6.3 and show only the inputs and outputs. Figure 6.4 is an example of the flip-flop circuit as a box.

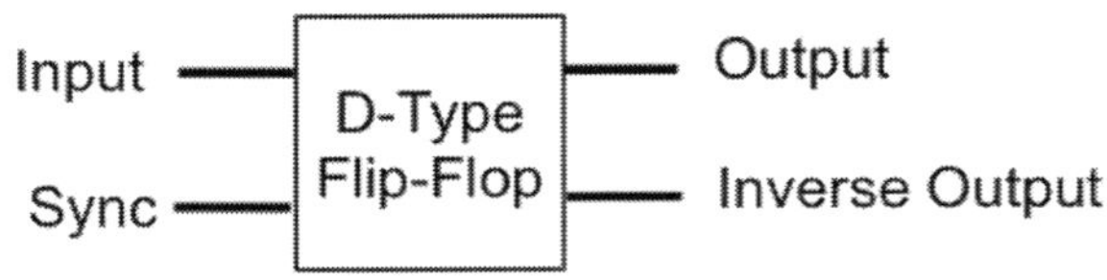

Figure 6.4. Encapsulated D-Type Flip-flop.

This simple flip-flop circuit is the basis for all memory in computing. As mentioned earlier, there are other variations of this circuit, but they all function basically the same way. The important point about this circuit is that it remembers the value we present at the input when we pulse the Sync input (sometimes the Sync input is called the *Clock* input). If we combine eight of these circuits in parallel, such that each of the parallel circuits has its own input and output, but share the same Sync line, we have a byte of memory.

If we connect even more of these coupled flip-flop circuits together to create a word, we call it a *register*. A register is just a word of memory that resides in the CPU. When a CPU executes an instruction, the control module retrieves a word from the memory external to the CPU and places the contents in a register called the instruction register. This is known as the fetch cycle of the instruction execution. With what we already know, we can imagine that the CPU accomplishes the fetch cycle using a series of multiplexors and demultiplexors to route the contents of memory to the register, followed by pulsing the register so that the register retains the value of the instruction from memory.

The ALU is connected to the instruction register, or at least the ALU is connected to several bits in the register. In our example ALU, these bits are the four controlling bits of the ALU (two invertor bits and two operation selection bits) such that the instruction in the instruction register indicates which operation the ALU will perform. Note that some of the CPU instructions may not involve the ALU at all (e.g., moving data to and from memory, etc.), so the instruction register would need an additional bit to indicate that the instruction uses the ALU. We would need to use this ALU indication bit to feed another multiplexor to enable the output from the ALU, much like we used the multiplexor within the ALU to choose the specific function. This description is a little nebulous. If it doesn't all make sense yet, we will explain this much more carefully a little later, but hopefully we are starting to visualize how CPU instruction execution takes place.

Besides the instruction register, the CPU has other general-purpose registers. These general-purpose registers act as inputs and outputs to the ALU. The CPU routes the contents of a general-purpose register using multiplexors based on bits of the instruction that indicate the inputs and the output.

As an example, imagine a 16-bit instruction where we use one bit to indicate if the instruction is an ALU instruction or not, and the next four bits for ALU configuration. This leaves 11 bits for specifying the inputs and output. If the CPU has eight general-purpose registers, we will require three bits to indicate one of the eight general purpose registers. We could use these three bits to drive a multiplexor to select from the eight registers. Since ALU instructions require two input registers and one output register, we can use nine bits of the instruction to indicate the registers – three for each of the three registers. Figure 6.5 shows an example of an ALU instruction format.

A	I	I	F	F	1	1	1	2	2	2	O	O	O	X	X

```
  A = ALU Enable
 II = ALU Input Invertor
 FF = ALU Function Selection
111 = Input Register 1
222 = Input Register 2
OOO = Output Register
 XX = Unused
```

Figure 6.5. An Example ALU Instruction Format.

Given three of the components we understand, registers, multiplexors and demultiplexors, we can now design a complete register bank. For example, we might design a register bank of eight 16-bit registers. For eight registers, we need three control lines for our multiplexor and demultiplexor. We can connect all the register inputs in parallel such that bit zero of each register is connected, bit one of each register is also connect, bit two is connected, etc. We use a demultiplexor with the outputs connected to the clock signal of the registers to allow the CPU to determine which register to write to. We use the multiplexor on the output-side of the registers to determine which register we want to read from. Figure 6.6 shows this configuration.

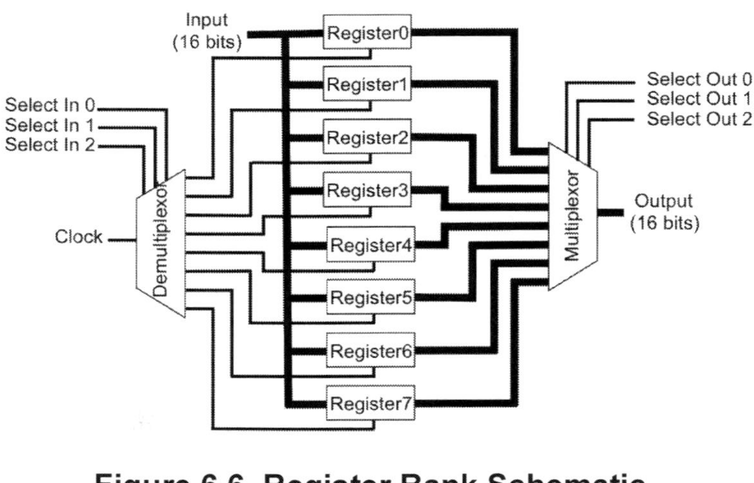

Figure 6.6. Register Bank Schematic.

The thick lines in Figure 6.6 represent the data path consisting of 16 parallel lines. The thin lines represent single lines. These connect to the Clock signal of each register. We can also use the three thin lines to select which register to write to or read from. We can use this same idea to create the computer's Random Access Memory (RAM). Memory works the same way, but with more registers and larger multiplexors/demultiplexors.

It appears that the general shape of our CPU is starting to emerge, but there are a couple more sequential components we need to understand before we will have all the tools we need to completely design a CPU. The need for the first of these additional components becomes apparent when we think about the Clock input of the registers. The question is, what drives the pulse for the Clock input?

Notice that all the bits in a register would all need the Clock input at the same time. In addition to bits within a single register, multiple registers may need to have the Clock input occur at the same time. For example, the instructions described in Figure 6.5 require two input registers. These input registers must receive the Clock input at the same time in order for the result to reflect the operation based on both inputs. There must also be a relationship between the timing of the input registers and the output register – the output register must receive the Clock pulse immediately after the pulse for the inputs. Further, we can imagine the other instructions (not yet explained) that move data and instructions to/from memory. These instructions also require specific synchronization.

Clock

Because of these timing requirements, it makes sense to have a general synchronization mechanism that applies throughout the computer – a global drumbeat that allows the computer to synchronize all operations. The component that emits the global drumbeat is called the *clock*. A computer's clock alternates outputting a 0 and a 1 at regular intervals.

We can see intuitively that a clock's circuit must have a feedback loop since the next output depends on its previous state. The schematic for a clock circuit is easy to draw, but is a bit confusing to understand. Figure 6.7 shows a clock schematic.

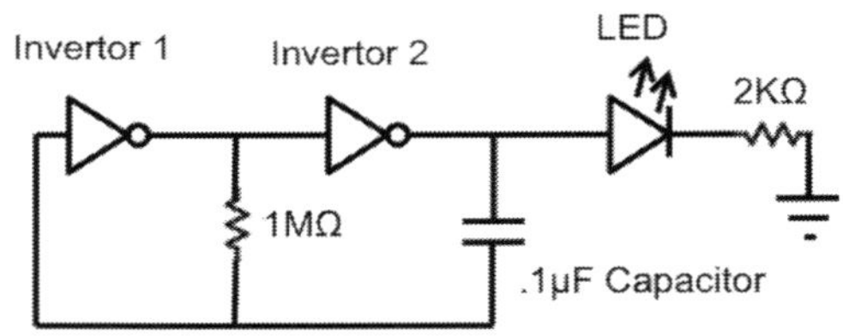

Figure 6.7. A Clock Circuit Schematic.

The clock circuit in Figure 6.7 outputs a signal, as indicated by the LED, that alternates by being on for a short period (about a quarter of a second) and then off for the same amount of time. Actual computer clocks alternate much more quickly, but we have slowed this circuit down so that we can see the LED blink.

While it may be entertaining to see the LED blink, the blinking LED is not so much the point as it is *how* the circuit makes the LED blink. This circuit introduces a couple of things we have not yet seen. The first is a symbol on the far right end of the circuit consisting of three horizontal lines of diminishing length. This is a symbol for *ground*, which merely means the line connects to the negative pole of the power supply.

The second new symbol is two horizontal lines in the middle of the schematic and has the label ".1µF Capacitor". This symbol represents a *capacitor*. The actual capacitor hardware looks like a small (often yellowish-brown) rounded disk with two wires. The purpose of a capacitor is to store up charge. We measure the amount of charge a capacitor can hold (its capacitance) using units known as Farads. We see in Schematic 6.7 that the capacitor holds one tenth of one microfarad.

The other symbols in the schematic are familiar to us. We see two invertor gates, an LED and a couple of resistors.

Unlike the logic circuits from previous chapters, this circuit is a bit tricky to understand because of its feedback loop. In order to understand this circuit, let's start by assuming we have a logical input of 0 to Invertor 1. If this were the case, Invertor 1 would output a logical 1. In turn, Invertor 2 would have a logical output of 0. So far, this seems simple enough, but in order to understand this circuit, we need to realize that the logical values of 0 and 1 correspond to voltage levels of 0 and 5 Volts respectively.

When Invertor 1 outputs 5 Volts, then the current flows through the 1MΩ resistor and begins to charge the capacitor. The capacitor acts like a bucket and soaks up the charge for a while in such a way that the input to Invertor 1 remains at 0 Volts. Eventually, the capacitor absorbs as much charge as it can. When the capacitor becomes full, then the current builds up at the input to Invertor 1 until this voltage finally reaches the threshold for Invertor 1, then Invertor 1 changes its output from 5 volts to 0 volts. When this change occurs, Invertor 2 also changes and begins to output 5 Volts (a logical 1). This new output of Invertor 2 affects the capacitor by immediately raising the voltage level of both sides of the capacitor. Meanwhile, the 0 Volts output by Invertor 1 causes the capacitance to drain from the capacitor, which maintains a logical 1 input to Invertor 1 for a period of time. Eventually, the capacitor drains enough that the Voltage input to Invertor 1 drops below the threshold and Invertor 1, once again, outputs 5 Volts and the cycle starts over.

Wow, that was a lot to try to understand! If the previous explanation is too confusing, we can simplify our view of the circuit by thinking of the capacitor as a tank of water. When the output of Invertor 1 is a logical 1, the tank is filling. The tank fills until it reaches a high-water mark. Reaching the high-water mark causes Invertor 1 to switch from an output of logical 1 to an output of logical 0, which also causes the tank to start draining. When the tank drains to a point where it reaches the low-water mark, Invertor 1 changes its output back to logical 1, which causes the tank to start filling again.

The 1MΩ resistor near the middle of the schematic determines how fast the capacitor fills. The larger the resistor, the slower the capacitor fills. We have used a very large resistor in order to slow the osculation of the circuit so that we can see the LED blink. We could speed up the blinking by using a smaller resistor. Or, we can slow the blinking down by adding additional resistance by placing more resistors in series.

Similarly, if we want to affect the speed of the blinking, we can increase the capacitance we use. Unlike resistance, which we increase by adding in series, we increase capacitance by adding more capacitors in parallel. Try it out. Build the circuit and add more resistance and more capacitance to see the blinking slow down. Notice that the rate of blinking is related to the amount of resistance and capacitance. The formula is:

$$\text{Time} = \text{Resistance} \times \text{Capacitance}$$

We can use this clock circuit to drive all the components within the CPU that need a regular pulse.

Counter

The final sequential circuit we need to understand before we can put it all together in a CPU is a circuit that controls the sequence of operations in the CPU. Each CPU instruction requires several phases of execution to complete its work. In the first phase, the processor fetches the next instruction from memory. In the second phase, the processor decodes the instruction and fetches the operands. Next the processor executes the operation, followed by the processor storing the result of the operation in a register. Finally, the processor updates the program counter to point at the next instruction. The number of phases may vary from processor to processor, but they follow this general form.

At the heart of the circuitry that controls these phases of instruction execution is a component called a counter. A counter consists of a series of flip-flops. Each flip-flop has its inverse output connected back to its input so that on each clock cycle, the output of the flip-flop alternates between one and zero. We connect the first flip-flop in the series to the clock so that the flip-flop changes its output on each clock cycle.

We connect the output of the first flip-flop to the clock input on the second flip-flop so that the second flip-flop alternates ones and zeros at half the rate of the first. We can connect a third flip-flop to the second in a similar manner so that the third flip-flop oscillates at half the speed of the second and one quarter the speed of the first.

If we also connect the outputs from each flip-flop to an LED, and organize the LEDs so that the output from the first flip-flop is on the far right, the second is in the middle and the third is on the far left, we see an interesting pattern. We can interrupt this pattern as binary counting. The far right LED is the ones position of the binary number, the middle LED is the twos position and the left LED is the fours position. Figure 6.8 shows a schematic for a three-bit counter.

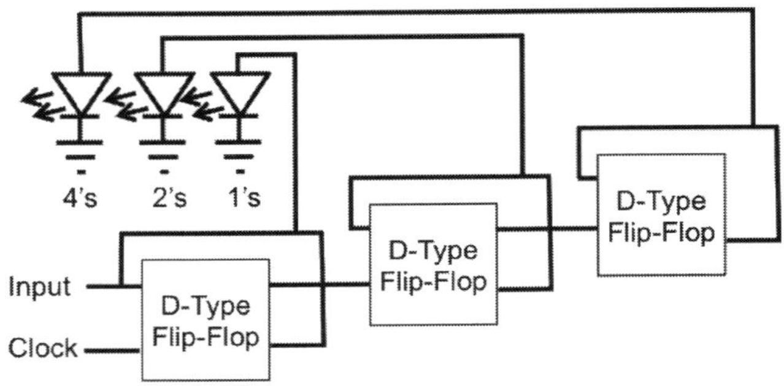

Figure 6.8. Three-Bit Counter Schematic.

We can continue to cascade flip-flops together to create a counter that counts to as large of a number as we would like. We can use the output from the counter as the control lines of a multiplexor. This combination of a counter and a multiplexor allow us to move through the various phases of instruction execution, as we will see in the coming chapter.

The counter circuit, along with clock and the register circuits comprise all of the sequential circuits we need to build a complete CPU. In the next chapter we will look at putting this all together.

Project: Build Bits, Registers and Counters

First, let's build the circuit for a single flip-flop as shown in Figure 6.3. If we have 2 7400s we can use all NAND gates like Figure 6.3. Alternatively, if we have a single 7400 and a 7404, we can replace two of the NAND gates with two NOT gates. We should build the flip-flop and convince ourselves we understand how it works.

The materials for the circuit in Figure 6.3 include the following:

- 1 breadboard
- 1 power source (either a wall wart or a battery supply pack)
- 1 7400 IC (4 NAND gates)
- 1 7404 IC (2 NOT gates)
- 2 LED
- 2 1KΩ resistor
- 2 pushbutton switches
- 12 jumper wires

Next, let's return to Logisim to build a 16-bit register. However, if we want to use Logisim to simulate circuits, we need to be aware of a shortcoming. Logisim has a bug in it that prevents us from using our own D-type flip-flop (built from NAND gates) within a feedback loop. Fortunately, Logisim provides its own implementation of a D-type flip-flop that works correctly in feedback loops. Therefore, if we need to simulate a D-type flip-flop within a larger circuit, we will need to use the Logisim implementation.

Once we understand how to build a register out of flip-flops, we can use Logisim's built-in register along with Logisim's multiplexors and demultiplexors to build a bank of registers. At this point it becomes important to learn to use Logisim's cables if you have not already done so.

Next, go back the breadboard and build a clock. Experiment with changing the resistance and the capacitance to vary the clock cycle time. You can use the circuit in Figure 6.7. The materials for the circuit in Figure 6.7 include the following:

- 1 breadboard
- 1 power source (either a wall wart or a battery supply pack)
- 1 7404 IC (2 NOT gates)
- 1 LED
- 1 2KΩ resistor
- 1 1MΩ resistor

- 1 .1μF capacitor
- 7 jumper wires

Finally, using Logisim's D-type flip-flops, build a counter that can count from zero to seven. You can use Logisim's output component to see the value, or for an interesting challenge you can connect the output lines to a Hex display. You can drive the counter with a button, or you may want to tryout using the built-in Logisim clock component.

Once you have successfully built each of these projects, you are ready to put it all together into a computer. In the next chapter, we will do just that!

We take all the components we have built in previous chapters and combine them to create a fully functional computer. As a result of this chapter we will understand how machine language affects a CPU, as well as how microcode controls the various components of the CPU.

Chapter 7 – The Processor

In this chapter we will look at how to use all the components we have developed along the way to design a fully functional CPU. Let's review the list of components we have accumulated to this point. The list includes:

- N-bit NOT
- N-bit AND
- N-bit OR
- N-bit Adder
- N-bit Shifter
- NXM Multiplexor
- NXM Demultiplexor
- N-bit ALU
- N-bit Registers
- Clock
- N-bit Counter

We saw in previous chapters, that the ALU provides addition, subtraction, ANDing, ORing, NORing and shifting. Many processors handle shifting outside of the ALU, but we put shifting in ours. In addition to the ALU operations, our CPU needs to be able to do two more operations. These operations have the names *load* and *store*. The load operation moves a value, either from memory or a constant, into a register. The store operation moves a value from a register to memory. Given these two final operations, our CPU will be completely capable of running any program. Other processors might have additional instructions that ours does not. These additional instructions might be more convenient or quicker ways of doing things that might take our CPU a few more instructions to perform, but in terms of computability, our processor will be complete.

Before we try to figure out the circuitry for our CPU, let's consider what instructions we will want to execute. As we discussed previously, we will need ALU instructions that will perform arithmetic and logical operations. These ALU operations will operate using the CPU's general-purpose registers as inputs and outputs. In addition to the ALU instructions, we need a way initialize registers with constant values as well as move values between registers and memory.

Besides the ALU, constant register value and memory/register movement instructions, we will also need an instruction to allow us to branch our code based on conditions. For example, we may want to create a loop by incrementing a counter variable in our code and branching back to the beginning of the loop until the counter variable reaches some maximum. For our CPU, we will use one of the general-purpose registers as the *program counter*, say register 0. The program counter (PC) keeps track of the location in memory of the next instruction to execute. So if we want the CPU to branch, all we need to do is to move the value of the branch into register 0 based on some condition.

Let's summarize the instructions we want our CPU to have.

- ALU operation
- Load a value from memory to a register
- Load a constant value to a register
- Store a value from a register to a location in memory
- Move a value from one register to another conditionally

Appendix C shows the binary encoding for each of these instructions.

Even though we have created a set of digital components as described in the list at the beginning of the chapter, trying to figure out how to build a processor can still be a very complicated and confusing task. It's worth taking just a few minutes at this point to try to think about how we might do this. If we just take each of the instructions from our instruction set and try to implement the circuitry to facilitate the instruction, we will probably quickly become overwhelmed. So, how will we ever fight our way through the processor design?

The secret to simplifying the processor design is in how we think about the design. It doesn't work as well to think about individual instructions yet. Instead, let's first think about the major pieces of the computer. These pieces include:

- ALU
- Register bank
- Instruction register
- Control logic
- Memory

With the exception of the control logic, we have investigated each of these components, and we understand what they do, how they work and what each of their inputs and outputs are. Let's start by laying these out on a schematic. We won't connect them yet; we will just position them so we can start to think about their connections. Figure 7.1 shows this layout.

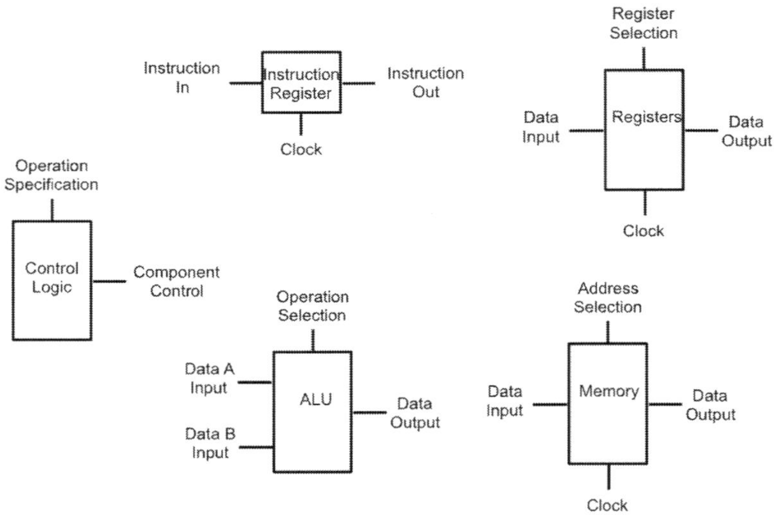

Figure 7.1. Computer Components Layout.

Figure 7.1 shows the initial layout of all of the five major components we will have in our computer. Notice that each component shows its inputs and outputs as a single line. In actuality, these individual lines represent many parallel inputs and outputs – much like a cable. But we'll keep the description simple by showing many wires as a single line. We will make other decisions that will also emphasize simplicity and clarity in our CPU design. This will make our processor a little slower than production processor designs, but the purpose of our design is to understand how processors work, so we are less worried about performance.

What's the next step in our processor design? We might be tempted to take a single component and wire it up, but that is also a relatively complicated approach. Instead, let's think about how data flows through the processor. This means that we will, for now, ignore the control lines of the processor.

Maybe the most straightforward data flow to consider occurs on every instruction. Remember that after every instruction we will need to increment the program counter (register 0). This means that we will take the output from the registers, run it through an incrementer and store it back in the registers. To simplify our thinking, let's introduce a handful of helper internal registers. These register are not strictly necessary and will slow down our processor performance some, but they will make it easy for us to conceptualize the processor design. We will use one of these internal registers to hold the incoming data. We will use another register to hold the out-going data and we will use a third register to hold the selected register address.

By configuring the internal registers this way, when we want to get a value from any general-purpose register, we would load the internal register selector (a three-bit register) with the register number and then clock the outgoing register to hold onto the data. Similarly, to change the value of a general-purpose register, we would load the incoming data into the internal input register, next we would load the register number into the register selection and finally pulse the general-purpose registers' clock to update the register.

Using these internal helper registers adds a few extra steps in our instruction execution, but these registers make it much easier to think about and debug our design. In fact, these helper registers are so useful, that we will add them to several other components. Figure 7.2 shows the computer layout with the helper registers.

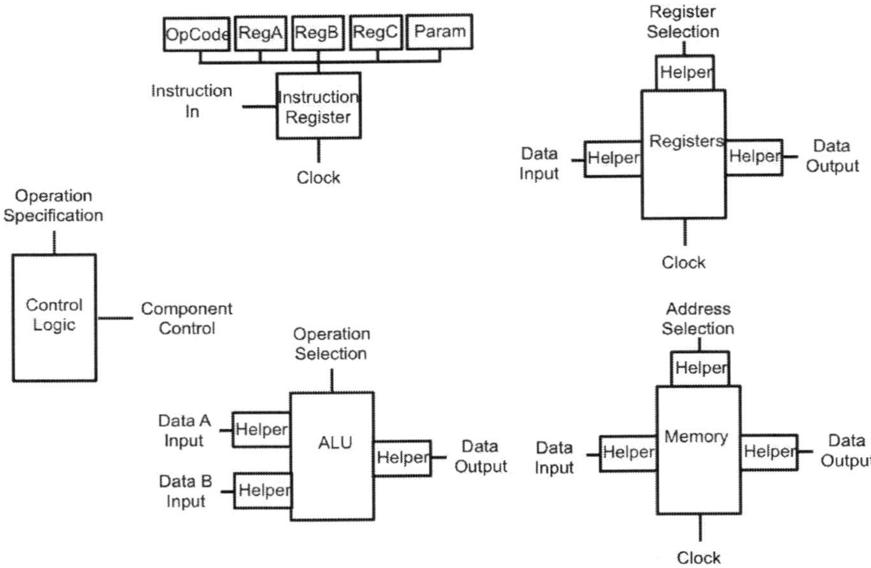

Figure 7.2. Computer Component with Helper Buffer Layout.

In Figure 7.2 we also added some additional registers associated with the instruction register. These registers hold the values of each of the pieces of the instruction. The OpCode helper register holds the first five bits of the instruction, the RegA holds the next three bits, as does RegB and RegC respectively. The Param helper register holds the last eight bits of the instruction. We will show how this is helpful shortly.

Next, let's consider the data flow of each of the instructions. We can start with ALU instructions. Notice that all ALU instructions receive input from general-purpose registers. Notice also that the ALU outputs to general-purpose registers. So we will need a path from the output of the registers to the inputs of the ALU. We will also need a path from the ALU output to the input of the registers.

The instructions that move data to and from memory will require paths between the memory and the registers. We will also require a path between the Param helper register and the general-purpose registers. The Param helper register contains any constant we may want to move to a general-purpose register. The Param helper register only holds eight bits, so we will need to extend the constant with an additional eight zeros.

Since we included the Param path, let's also include paths between each of the RegX (i.e., RegA, RegB, RegC) helper registers and the Register Selection helper register. These paths allow us to use bits from the instruction to indicate general-purpose registers we want to use when executing instructions.

The final data path we need is from memory to the instruction register. This path lets us fetch instructions from memory for execution.

A couple of these paths converge to the same input. For example, the Register Selection register receives input from all of the possible positions in the instruction. Also, the Data Input register for the register bank also receives input from several locations. When this occurs we should use a multiplexor to decide which input to use. Figure 7.3 shows the layout with these data paths with the multiplexors.

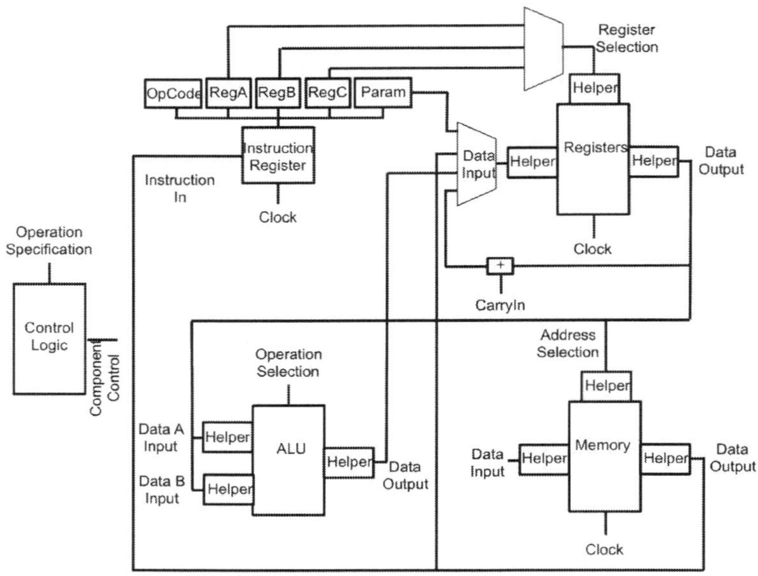

Figure 7.3. Computer Component Layout with Data Paths and Multiplexors.

Now that we have the data paths in place, just about all we have left to do is to control the flow of the data. This is the job of the Control Logic component. The Control Logic component plays traffic cop by getting input mainly from the OpCode, and controlling the operations of the multiplexors and clock signals of the various registers and memory. To diagram all these connections would get a bit messy, so we won't show all the control connections. Instead, let's look at how the Control Logic works and it should become clear how to make the connections.

The control logic is in charge of what we will refer to as *microcode*. As we have alluded to many times throughout this book, CPU instructions actually require many smaller steps. Each of these steps moves data from one place in the CPU or memory to another. These steps form a micro-program.

Let's think about how an ALU instruction proceeds. The first thing this program needs to do is to fetch the instruction from memory. To fetch the instruction, we need to set the register selection helper register to point at the program counter (register 0). Then we can load the Data Output helper register with the address of the next instruction. We place this address in the Address Selection register and load the instruction into the Memory Data Output register. We move the instruction to the instruction register and decode the instruction.

Unlike regular programs, micro-programs can be very concurrent – multiple things can happen at the same time. So, while we are doing the last few operations we just described, we can also increment the value in the Register Data Output and send the result back into the Register Data Input and finally back into register 0. This has the effect of incrementing the program counter and can occur at the same time as the rest of the operation preparation.

At this point of execution in our example ALU instruction, we have decoded the instruction and we can determine that the instruction is an ALU operation by inspecting the high-order bit of the instruction. All the micro-steps up to this point are the same for every instruction, but now the microcode diverges based on the specific instruction.

For the ALU instruction, we route the input to the ALU from the registers specified in RegA and RegB of the decoded instruction. We do this by setting the Register Selection value based on RegA (and later on RegB) and loading the result into the general-purpose register Data Output. Then we can load the data into the Data A Input on the ALU. We do the same steps to load Data B Input. The ALU operation receives its operation orders from the OpCode register of the decoded instruction. This path between the OpCode register and the ALU is a direct connection, so as soon as the instruction is decoded, the ALU begins performing the specified operation. Once the Control Logic presents the appropriate input, the correct result appears at the ALU's Data Output where the control logic loads the data into the ALU's output helper register. Finally, the control logic loads the Register Selection with the value in RegC, loads the ALU result into the registers Data Input, and clocks the data into the specified general-purpose register.

As a side note, the astute reader will notice a problem at the beginning of this description when reading and writing to/from the program counter. How do we specify the program counter to the Register Selection register? One way is to add another input to the multiplexor that is all zeros and select this input when we want to select the program counter. In fact, we address the program counter often enough that is makes sense to make this the default value of the multiplexor so that if we do not specify otherwise, we get the value of the program counter.

The description of the microcode algorithm is intricate and may require careful study to understand. Let's try and summarize it more like code. Here are the six (0 through 5) common steps for all instructions:

0 – Select the PC as the input for register selection and load the register selection register
1 – Load the register's Data Output register
2 – Turn on the CarryIn at the incrementer, Load the register's Data Input and load the memory's Address Selection
3 – Clock the general-purpose registers and load the memory's Data Output
4 – Load the Instruction Register
5 – Decode the Instruction into the sub-field registers

Here are the nine (0 through 8) ALU specific steps of the instruction:

0 – Select the multiplexor for input from RegA and load the Register Selection
1 – Load the register's Data Output
2 – Load the ALU's Data A Input
3 – Select the multiplexor for input from RegB and load the Register Selection
4 – Load the register's Data Output
5 – Load the ALU's Data B Input
6 – Select the multiplexor for input from RegC and load the Register Selection, also load the ALU's Data Output
7 – Select the multiplexor for input from the ALU and load the register's Data Input
8 – Clock the result into the general-purpose registers

How does the control logic cause these steps to occur? Since there is a time sequence to these micro-steps, we realize that we will need to use a clock circuit that oscillates between zero and one as we have previously described. We use the output of the clock circuit as input to a counter. Then we can take the output from the counter and use it as the selector for a demultiplexor. We connect the data input of the demultiplexor to a constant one. By doing this, each output line of the demultiplexor pulses in sequence at the rhythm of the clock. Each of these output lines represents a different micro-code instruction in the sequence. Finally, we can run each of these lines through a demultiplexor to select lines based on the OpCode. In this way, we effectively have one line for each instruction of each OpCode.

In our ALU instruction example, we listed 15 micro-steps. Our counter will need to count to a value that is a power of two. The nearest value larger than 15 is 16, so we will make our control logic have 16 different micro-code states. What do we do with the extra state? We will just ignore the state and leave it unused. This is a bit wasteful. Production processors would not do this, but we aren't worried about optimization – just understanding how a processor works. In fact, production processor designers would work hard to cut the number of control logic states as these directly affect the speed of the processor. We can see that if we had not introduced the helper registers, that our instructions would be much faster. But these helper registers make the microcoding more discrete and hopefully easier.

All of this microcode description may seem a little abstract; so let's take a look at the form of the schematic for the control logic. Figure 7.4 shows this form for the control logic.

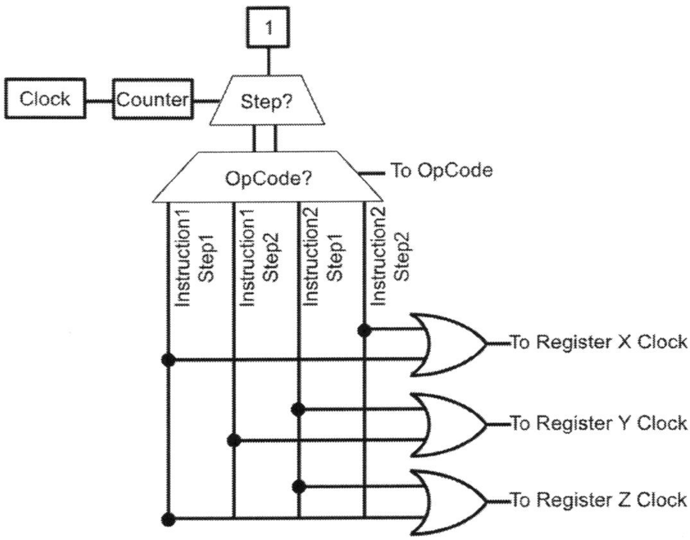

Figure 7.4. Control Logic Form Schematic.

In the schematic show in Figure 7.4, the control logic would control a CPU with two instructions and two micro-steps per instruction. In this example, step 1 of instruction 1 would cause the clock on register X and register Z to pulse. On step 2 of instruction 1, the clock on register Y would pulse. Similarly for instruction 2, step 1 would pulse the clocks on registers Y and Z, while step 2 would pulse the clock on register X.

Once we see the form, it becomes manageable to microcode the control logic. It's a bit tedious, but with patience we can work our way through it. We see that each line represents an instruction/step, and that we can cause certain things to happen by connecting the line, through an OR gate, to the appropriate clock line. Similarly, the lines can drive the selection for multiplexors.

There is little doubt that this work can be tedious and error prone. One way to avoid errors is to first write down the microcode steps as we showed previously. After we write these steps down, we can desk-check our work until we think we have the micro-algorithm right. Then we can go about the task of wiring our circuit according to the algorithm.

One of the nice things about having all the helper registers is that we can have our microcode move data around and then check to make sure we have the right data in the right places. This is enormously helpful when trying to debug our processor. Debugging can be very complicated because, when things don't work quite right, we can't be sure if the problem is with the data path, the control path or the control logic. So when we first put our processor together, it requires patience as we work out the kinks. But take heart – we can indeed work our way through it!

There is one last item that we need to mention before we are completely ready to complete our CPU design. This item has to do with conditional branching. We intend to use our register-to-register move instruction to do the conditional branching. The data path can use the same path we use to increment the program counter, but we won't turn on the incrementer so that we get a straight copy. The question we must answer is: how do we affect the conditional aspect of the move operation?

We will make the move operation conditional on the result of the most recent ALU operation. Notice that we can compare two values by subtracting the values and inspecting the result.

For example, if we subtract value A from value B and the result is positive, we know that A is greater than B. Similarly if the result is negative, then we know that A is less than B, and if the result is zero, we know that A equals B. With twos-complement binary representation, determining if a value is negative is as easy as checking the high-order bit. If the high-order bit is zero but at least one other bit in the value is set, the value is positive. Obviously, if no bits are set, the value is zero. We can translate this logic into a circuit that inspects the results of an ALU operation and sets a three-bit register to indicate the disposition of the result. The high-order bit indicates we will accept a negative result. The low-order bit indicates a positive result and the middle bit indicates a zero result.

When we perform the register-to-register move operation, we use the value in RegA as the source register. We use the value in RegB as the destination. This leaves RegC unused. We can use the three bits in RegC to indicate which results are acceptable from the most recent ALU operation. We follow the same pattern as that described for the ALU result disposition. Therefore, we can AND the value of RegC with the ALU result register. If the result of the AND is non-zero, we set a line to 1 to tell the control logic to execute the instruction.

The control logic merely ANDs-in this conditional signal with the lines for the conditional instruction steps. If the conditional line is low, the instruction does not get executed. If the conditional line is high, then the control logic executes the steps of the conditional instruction.

Note that in either case, the instruction must perform at least part of the instruction to increment the program counter. Since several of the steps of each instruction are the same, it may be helpful to form another set of lines in the control logic that represents these common micro-steps. This will eliminate some redundant circuitry.

So there you have it. We have explained how to design our own CPU. We have left out a few minor details for individual discovery, but we have seen all the major brush strokes. This chapter is a lot to digest, but if we take it slowly, we will see that designing a CPU is not all that mysterious.

Our journey in this book has taken us all the way from a simple circuit that lights an LED, to how transistors work, to how to build NAND gates from transistors, to how to use NAND gates to build all Boolean logic, to how to use Boolean logic to build binary logic, to how to use Boolean logic to save state, to how to use these constructs to build CPU subcomponents, and finally to how to completely configure a CPU. Our journey required a lot of steps, but as we look back, we see that each step, by itself, was easy. But the best part of our journey is that now we know exactly how a computer works!

Project: Build a Computer

Let's use Logisim to design a complete CPU and associated memory. As a result of the previous projects, we now understand how all the basic building blocks work. So for this project let's use any of the Logisim components available. Notice, for example, that Logisim provides a memory component. We can also use Logisim's registers, multiplexors and demultiplexors as well as N-way Boolean gates. Besides the Logisim components we can also re-use the ALU we have already built.

We can follow the steps described in this chapter. First we will layout the five major components. Then we can connect the data path. When we start to connect these components, it will be much easier if we learn to use Logisim's cables. Cables are connections of wires. We can select individual wires of a cable by using Logisim's splitters. Finally, we will build the control logic as described and connect up the control lines.

This chapter has left a lot of design work for us to do. Unlike previous chapters that spelled out most of the design, this chapter used broad-brush strokes, but has left some of the challenge, and hence the thrill, of figuring out the processor design. This leaves us some freedom to make our CPU as sophisticated as we like. The instructions in Appendix C may be a good place to start, but if we feel confident, we may want to add more instructions or even optimize our design.

Once we have a CPU design, we can write a machine language program to try out our computer. Our program should try out each of our instructions. For example, we might write a program that loops and increments a variable in memory. If we use Logisim's memory component, we can load Hex values directly into memory. We can also save the memory contents to a file for convenience.

This is a great project! Once we complete this project we not only feel the satisfaction of having completed an interesting and challenging project, but we also have a sound understanding of computer architecture. We will be surprised at how many ways this understanding will enrich our ability to work with computers. So, enjoy this final project!

Appendix A – Boolean Fundamentals

Boolean logic, named for Charles Boole, an English Logician, is the basis for all computational logic. This appendix describes the fundamental concepts of Boolean logic used in this book.

Boolean logic deals with only two values: true and false. Sometimes we represent these values as 1 and 0. This mapping to 1 and 0 allows us to relate Boolean functions to binary functions.

There are three fundamental functions in Boolean logic. These functions are

- NOT
- AND
- OR

The NOT operation is unary (requires only one input), while AND and OR are binary operations (requiring two operands). These functions have specific definitions. We will represent these functions using truth tables. Truth tables show the inputs and outputs using a columnar form. Here are the truth tables for each of these fundamental functions.

NOT

Input	**Output**
False	True
True	False

AND

Input A	Input B	Output
False	False	False
False	True	False
True	False	False
True	True	True

OR

Input A	Input B	Output
False	False	False
False	True	True
True	False	True
True	True	True

We can use these functions to form expressions, and we can use expressions to create equations. For example, we can represent the NOT of a value by placing a line over it as follows:

$$\overline{A}$$

Further, we can create an expression that evaluates to true if and only if the inputs A and B are true. We would write this expression as

$$A \cdot B$$

The dot between the A and B means AND. Similarly, we can write A OR B as the following expression.

$$A + B$$

We see that these expressions look similar to normal mathematical algebraic expressions. This is intentional because many of the properties that apply to mathematical algebra also apply to Boolean algebra. These properties include Commutativity and Associativity.

Commutativity means that the following expressions are equivalent:

$$A + B = B + A$$

and

$$A \cdot B = B \cdot A$$

Associativity means that the following expressions are equivalent:

$$(A + B) + C = A + (B + C)$$

and

$$(A \cdot B) \cdot C = A \cdot (B \cdot C)$$

However, like in mathematical algebra, associativity does not imply that mixed expressions are equivalent as shown in the following:

$$(A + B) \cdot C \neq A + (B \cdot C)$$

We can use a distributive property to convert expressions such as the following:

$$A \cdot (B + C) = (A \cdot B) + (A \cdot C)$$

The distributed property also provides for:

$$A + (B \cdot C) = (A + B) \cdot (A + C)$$

Besides Commutativity, Associativity and Distributivity, we can use De Morgan's laws to perform Boolean algebraic manipulations. These laws provide the following equivalence:

$$\overline{A \cdot B} = \overline{A} + \overline{B}$$

Which is to say that the NOT of A AND B is equivalent to the NOT of A OR the NOT of B. In addition, De Morgan's laws provide for:

$$\overline{A + B} = \overline{A} \cdot \overline{B}$$

For the work you will do in this book, these are all the axioms you will need to know. Using these axioms, you can manipulate expressions into forms that may be handier or may optimize the number of gates you will need for your schematics.

Appendix B – Binary Number Systems

Most of the modern programming languages use types like integers and floating-point numbers. When we use modern higher-level languages, we usually don't need to concern ourselves with the how the computer represents these numbers, but for machine and assembly language it is very important to understand these representations. This appendix explains how computers represent various types of numbers.

The foundation for representation in a computer is the binary value. We call the numbers we normally use *decimal* numbers in which we use digits of zero through nine to represent values. We might also say that decimal numbers are base-ten numbers or have a radix of ten. This is because each digit in a decimal number represents a power of ten.

Let's look at an example. Consider the number 123. In the number 123, the '1'digit represents one hundred, the '2' represents 2 tens and the three represents 3 ones.To put it another way, the '3' represents 3×10^0, the '2' represents 2×10^1 and the '1' represents 1×10^2. If we had more digits in front of the '1', they would represent $N \times 10^3$, and so forth. We see that the place of the digit in the number represents the number of the power of ten. Hence, the radix of the number is ten.

Computers represent numbers using a radix of two. We call radix two numbers *binary* numbers. These binary numbers work the same way decimal numbers do except that instead of using digits of zero through nine, we only use digits of zero and one. The place each digit represents a power of two, starting with the left most place - being 2^0. The digit just to the left represents 2^1, then 2^2 and so on.

We refer to the binary digits as *bits*. We also refer to the bits on the right side of the value as the *least significant* bits or *lower-order* bits and the bits on the left side of the value as the *most significant* bits or *higher-order* bits.

To convert a number from binary to decimal, take each binary digit, multiply it by the power of two represented by its place and sum all the products. For example, imagine we have a binary value of 101010 that we want to convert to decimal. We start with the least significant bit, which is the zero at the far right, and we multiply it by 2^0 to get zero. Then we take the next bit, which is a one, multiply it by 2^1 to get 2. After we have multiplied all the bits by their powers of two, we add up all the results as follows:

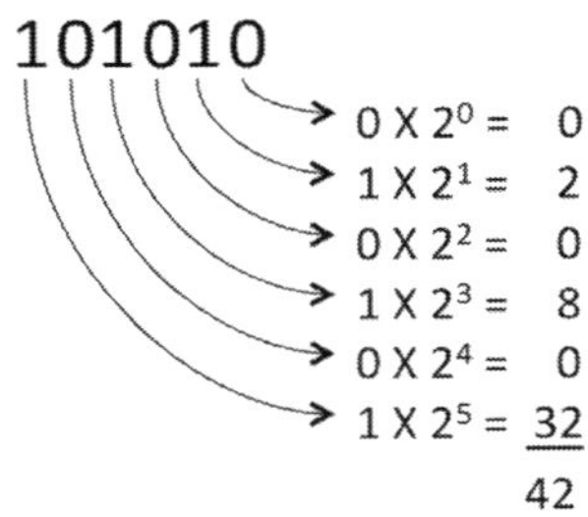

A byte contains eight bits, so a byte can represent the binary values of 00000000 through 11111111. In decimal, this means that a byte may represent values between 0 and 255, or a total of 256 different values.

10 bits can represent values of 0-1023 or 1024 different values. Since 1024 is approximately 1000 in decimal, it is a convenient value for us to use and we refer to this value as 1K. A two-byte value would have 16 bits and would be able to represent values on the range of 0-65535 or 65536 values. This is the same as 64 X 1024, so we call it 64K.

Likewise, 20 bits represents 1024 X 1024 and we refer to this as 1 Meg or 1M. Each time we increase our number by 10 bits, we add approximately three orders of magnitude in decimal and we have convenient names for these values. These are:

> 10 bits = 1K (Kilo)
> 20 bits = 1M (Mega)
> 30 bits = 1G (Giga)
> 40 bits = 1T (Tera)
> 50 bits = 1P (Peda)
> 60 bits = 1E (Exa)

Well, this seems fine as far as we have gone, but what about negative values? So far, the representations we have described are what are called *unsigned* values. To represent negative numbers we need *signed* values.

Effectively we use the highest bit to designate the value as positive or negative; a one if the value is negative and a zero for positive values. However, it gets a little more complicated than that. You see, negative numbers need to work so that when you add them to a positive number, they behave like they should. It turns out that in order to make negative numbers work correctly, instead of just using the highest bit as a sign bit, you also need to change other bits. The way we change the bits from positive to negative is called *twos complement*.

Getting the twos complement of a number is a two-step process. The first step is to perform a binary NOT operation on the value. The second step is to add one to the result of the first step.

For example, suppose we want the twos compliment of the value of a byte containing 42. The binary byte value for 42 would be 00101010. Remember that the first step is to perform a binary NOT operation. This means that we change all the ones to zeros and zeros to ones. The binary NOT of 42 is 11010101. The second step is to add one to this value as follows:

```
  11010101
+00000001
  11010110
```

Notice that the resultant byte has the high-order bit set to one. When we are looking at signed values, if the high-order bit is set to one, we know it is a negative number.

An interesting thing about twos compliment is that to undo the twos compliment operation we just perform the twos compliment again. For example, if we want to know what the decimal equivalent of the signed binary value 11010110 is, we perform the following steps:

1. Since the high order bit is set, we know the value is negative.
2. Since the value is negative, we take the twos compliment by:
    a. Taking the binary NOT of the value (in this case 00101001)
    b. Adding one to the value (which yields (00101010)
3. We then convert the binary value as though it were not signed (which gets us back to our original 42)

Finally, consider what happens when we add two bytes containing the values of 42 and -42. The value of 42 in binary is 00101010 and the value of -42 in binary is 11010110.

```
  00101010
+11010110
  00000000
```

Since a byte can only contain eight bits, the carry from the highest order bit gets dropped, but as we would expect, when we add 42 to -42, we get zero.

One last note about signed values – because we used the high-order bit for indicating sign, we can no longer represent values up to 255. Instead, the range of a signed byte is 127 to -128. We still have 256 different values, but the range has changed.

Appendix C – Example Instruction Set

This appendix describes an example CPU instruction set. The CPU we design in this book uses this instruction set. You may want to come up with your own instruction set. It's great to experiment! However, the description in the book will apply to the instructions we describe in this appendix.

Each instruction consists of 16 bits, however, not all instructions use all of the 16 bits. This appendix will specify the value of used bits with either a 0 or 1. This appendix shows unused bits as X.

Several fields comprise the 16 bits of each instruction. Generally these fields remain consistent across all instructions (the only exception is the "load constant" instruction). Let's first look at a general description of these fields, and then we will investigate each specific instruction.

Note that there are two general categories of instructions: ALU-based instructions and non-ALU instructions. If and only if the left-most bit of the instruction is 1, then the instruction is an ALU-based instruction.

Moving from left to right, the next four bits of the instruction form a field indicating the type of operation. If the operation is an ALU instruction, the first two bits of this four-bit field indicate inverting the A and B operands respectively. The last two bits of the four-bit field indicate the logical of arithmetic function (add, AND, OR or shift). If the instruction is not an ALU instruction, the four-bit field is an op-code field that specifies one of four operations: move memory to a register, move a constant to a register, move a register to memory or move a register to a register conditionally.

Immediately after the left-most five bits, there are three three-bit fields. These fields act as arguments to the various operations. All instructions use the first argument field, but only some instructions use the second or third fields. The meaning of these argument fields is instruction specific. One instruction, the move a constant to register instruction, only uses the first argument field and the last eight bits of the instruction represent an unsigned constant value.

Following is a detailed explanation of each instruction.

ALU Operation

Performs an arithmetic or logical operation.

15	14	13	12	11	10	9	8	7	6	5	4	3	2	1	0
1	N	N	F	F	A	A	A	B	B	B	C	C	C	X	X

Bit 15 - Constant 1 indicates ALU operation
Bits 14,13 – Invert the A and B operands
Bits 12,11 – ALU function:
- 00 – add the contents of registers A and B
- 01 – AND the contents of registers A and B
- 10 – OR the contents of registers A and B
- 11 – Shift the contents of register A by the value of register B

Bits 8-10 – Register A containing the input value
Bits 5-7 – Register B containing the input value
Bits 2-4 – Register C (the result register)
Bits 0,1 – Not used

Note: Inverting register B also adds one to the carry. So, inverting register B for an add function is equivalent to a twos complement subtraction of register B from register A.

Memory-to-Register Operation

Moves the content of memory to a register.

15	14	13	12	11	10	9	8	7	6	5	4	3	2	1	0
0	0	0	0	0	A	A	A	B	B	B	X	X	X	X	X

Bits 11-15 – Op-code 00000 indicates memory-to-register operation
Bits 8-10 – Destination register number
Bits 5-7 – Register number of the register containing the memory address
Bits 0-4 – Not used

Constant-to-Register

Moves an eight-bit constant value to the low-order bits of the destination register.

15	14	13	12	11	10	9	8	7	6	5	4	3	2	1	0
0	0	0	0	1	A	A	A	K	K	K	K	K	K	K	K

Bits 11-15 – Op-code 00001 indicates
constant-to-register operation
Bits 8-10 – Destination register number
Bits 0-7 – Eight-bit constant value

Note: Loading a 16-bit constant value requires loading two-eight bit values, shifting the high-order bits and ORing the two values together.

Register-to-Memory

Moves the content of a register to a specified memory address.

15	14	13	12	11	10	9	8	7	6	5	4	3	2	1	0
0	0	0	1	0	A	A	A	B	B	B	X	X	X	X	X

Bits 11-15 – Op-code 00010 indicates
register-to-memory operation
Bits 8-10 – Source register number
Bits 5-7 – Register containing the destination memory address
Bits 0-4 – Not used

Register-to-Register Conditional

15	14	13	12	11	10	9	8	7	6	5	4	3	2	1	0
0	0	0	1	1	A	A	A	B	B	B	N	Z	P	X	X

Bits 11-15 – Op-code 00011 indicates register-to-register conditional operation
Bits 8-10 – Source register number
Bits 5-7 – Destination register
Bits 2-4 – Conditional flags bits – operation will only occur if
N is set and previous ALU operation resulted in a negative value, OR
Z is set and previous ALU operation resulted in a zero value, OR
P is set and previous ALU operation resulted in a positive value.

Note: The flag bits may be combined to allow for less-than or equal, greater-than or equal, or not equal. Also, moving an address to register zero is equivalent to a branch instruction. The branch functionality may be combined with the conditional flags to provide conditional branching (if).

Index

Other Titles From Principle Publishing

The Alchemy of Computational Theory

For centuries alchemist tried to solve the elusive problem of turning lead into gold. They never really solved this problem, but the course of their experiments and research created the foundations for modern physics and many great discoveries. Attacking seemingly outlandish questions can yield valuable side effects.

Today, the outlandish question that many computer scientists are considering is: can a computer really be a mind?

In this book, Steve Halladay uses this question to motivate the exploration of concepts in computational theory and machine learning. So many courses on computational theory are dry and meaningless. These courses bludgeon the students with seemingly irrelevant proofs of obscure relationships. Ask most successful software engineers what they remember from their comp theory class and, more often than not, they will give you a blank stare. There is no reason for this! The concepts of computation theory speak to some of the most fascinating work in computer science today. It's just a matter of relating the theory to this exciting work. This book does just that!

In this book you will understand how theoretical computational machinery relates to bleeding edge software development. See how you can use finite state machines, pushdown automata and Turing machines to build intelligent interactive agents. Figure out what we can and cannot compute and realize what this says about how our minds work and what we are able to think. Explore machine learning and grasp how the theory of computation helps us understand the constraints of how quickly a machine can learn.

Getting a Clue with SQL

Learning SQL can be murder. Not the bludgeoning kind of murder most people experience when trying to learn the syntax and semantics of SQL, but a kinder, gentler side-splitting kind of murder as administered by Steve Halladay in this book. What is the motive? To make learning SQL enjoyable for you. What is the means? Halladay's relentless cheesy attempts at humor! What about the opportunity? Well, the opportunity is all yours as you learn how to query an SQL database by following Perry Hazard, a hapless recent college grad as he attempts to use SQL to solve a melodramatic murder mystery.

In this lampoon, the author drags you through the gory details of the SQL SELECT statement. You will learn all of the ins and outs as well as the relational theory that is the foundation of SQL. But don't let this book scare you. The reading may be fun, but the skills you learn from this book are deadly serious. The content is an edutainment odyssey format that has caused many to groan, "Halladay, you're killing me!" If, like most people, you want to solve a murder mystery and you have been dying to learn SQL, this book is for you!

Principle-Based Refactoring

You know good software when you see it, but how do you explain what good software is? Experienced software developers have pet practices and techniques that make their software easier to test, maintain and understand. But when you ask them how to make your software like theirs, they give you a seemingly endless list of rules. How can they remember all those rules? The secret is that they don't! Instead, experienced software developers understand a handful of basic principles. The rules are merely manifestations of these basic principles. But, principles are hard to explain; so experienced developers resort to explaining rules instead.

In Principle-Based Refactoring, Halladay explains a set of software refactoring rules and links the refactoring rules back to the basic principles that drive robust software design. The book identifies eight fundamental design principles and also includes a set of approximately fifty refactoring rules that illustrate the principles. Each rule has a summary description, a discussion, including references back to the driving principles, and examples of the rules' applications. In addition, this book discusses refactoring mechanics including test strategies that guide software developers in verifying the quality of refactored code.

Made in the USA
Columbia, SC
21 July 2021

42192591R00080